At Home with The Buckleys is one couple's take on the wild ride that is modern marriage, parenting and adulting. Told from both sides, James and Clair share a collection of hilarious stories and comedy excursions from their early lives, years of cult TV fame, having children and setting up their YouTube channel.

At Home With The Buckleys

At Home With The Buckleys

Scummy stories and misadventures from modern family life

James & Clair Buckley

RADAR

First published in Great Britain in 2022 by Radar, an imprint of
Octopus Publishing Group Ltd
Carmelite House
50 Victoria Embankment
London EC4Y 0DZ
www.octopusbooks.co.uk

An Hachette UK Company
www.hachette.co.uk

ISBN 978 1 80419 012 8

A CIP catalogue record for this book is available from the British Library.

Printed and bound in UK

1 3 5 7 9 10 8 6 4 2

This FSC® label means that materials used for the product have
been responsibly sourced.

This book, if you can call it that, is dedicated to you!
The amazing viewers of our YouTube channel, At Home
With The Buckleys. *What started as a spur of the moment,*
just for a laugh, insight into our lives has now become a little
community who we truly appreciate. We have had many
laughs together and hope to continue to do so.
Stay scummy guys!

Love, Clair & James

Contents

Introduction

Clair: We've been asked to write a book? Whose idea was that?

James: We haven't got anything to say!

Clair: Don't tell them that...

James: They'll work that out eventually!

Clair: Well we've managed to put together some bits and pieces that might be interesting?

James: Probably not.

Clair: No...probably not. If you like the vlogs, you might like it though?

James: No one likes the vlogs.

Clair: True.

James: Enjoy anyway!

1

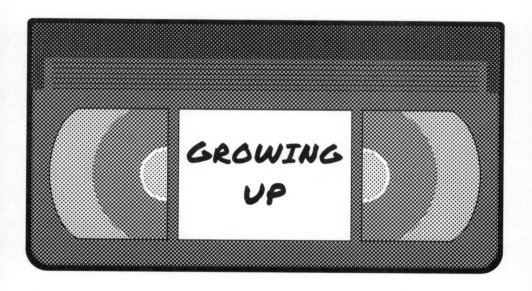

GROWING UP

Clair: I grew up in East Ayrshire, Scotland, in a small town in a valley. Where I grew up, it was a quiet little town and I loved it when I was young. It was such a wee, friendly place where everyone knew everybody (in a good way). Kilmarnock was the nearest bigger town and that was only 10 minutes away in the car. And that was where my mum and dad worked, at the Johnnie Walker whisky plant. Johnnie Walker was a big part of Kilmarnock and my parents weren't the only people in my life who worked there. My aunt did, my uncle did, my brother did for a while and lots of family friends did. So did I. For a short while after leaving secondary school, I got a job there to save up some money to fund my college nights out.

The bottling plant was attached to the factory floor and I worked on a couple of the stations (or lines) where you'd basically turn the whisky into a finished, nicely packaged product ready to go off to shops. My favoured line to work on was packing the bottles by hand and putting them in the boxes. You also had a line where you'd put the boxes together and add the dividers in, which was all right, but the worst one (which I hated and could not do, probably because I worked the night shift) was where you had to sit on a chair at a position where the conveyor belt curved and watch the bottles coming towards you and pull the ones where their labels weren't straight or the bottles had any imperfections. That was such a tough job to stay awake for because it was the kind of thing you actually imagine thinking of to send you to sleep! I used to get nudged by people when they saw I was dropping off, say 'Oh shit, sorry', but that would only keep me awake for a bit longer each time. And it didn't matter how much coffee I'd had, nothing seemed to work. So, if you've ever had a bottle of Johnnie Walker with a less than straight label, that may have been my fault. My friend Hannah, who also worked in Walker's, was a bit of a pro compared to me. She'd have her Lucozade and Pro Plus at the ready. She also used to bring in some food from a place called the Noodle Bar in Kilmarnock and we'd have a decent dinner to look forward to.

Not being the best employee in the world aside though, there is a strong connection to Johnnie Walker in my family and in my home town. It just so happens that James is a bit of a whisky lover, so he really won the jackpot when he met me and had an abundance of whisky on hand as well as from all my relatives who worked there.

The plant shut down in 2012 and it hit the town of Kilmarnock and the people employed in Walker's hard, including my parents.

★

When I got into my teens, my friends and I would sometimes venture into Glasgow for a night out and that would
take about 30–40 minutes from home. Loads of bands came
to play in Glasgow, which was amazing. It has a number of
legendary venues and I got to experience some amazing
nights. I genuinely believe that where I grew up was kind
of the perfect balance. You could go into the big city when
you wanted, but equally you could go to your little local
pub round the corner with your cousin for a quiet drink.

I went to the Metropolitan College in Glasgow as well,
which is when I got to know the city well and figured out
my favourite haunts. I studied art at college and met some
really great people during that time.

Most people think I'm from Glasgow and that's partly
because when I met James and got introduced to all sorts
of people down south, they'd ask me where I was from
and it was easier to say 'Glasgow' rather than 'I'm from
a little sleepy valley 10 minutes away from Kilmarnock,
which is about half hour from Glasgow.' You just pick the
nearest big city and go with that.

Music has always been such an important part of my life.
When I was 11 or 12, my dad, Davie, encouraged me to
listen to this band and that on his old record player. His
favourite bands were The Jam, The Who, Small Faces
and a little four-piece called The Beatles. I remember
him handing me a bunch of albums by The Jam, who are
his number one, absolute favourite band. (Paul Weller is
a hero genius in our house.) He said, 'Go listen to them.'

And when I did, I thought it was the best thing I'd ever heard. That was the moment that I fell in love with music.

But although I loved music, I didn't grow up wanting to be *in* music. I actually wanted to be an actress when I was little. I adored Winona Ryder and she was in films I loved, like *Edward Scissorhands* (1990) and *Dracula* (1992). She was different, took on more unconventional roles and got up to all sorts of crazy stuff. I loved Drew Barrymore for the same reasons. The film *Charlie's Angels* (2000) was a big thing for me, aged 12, seeing Cameron Diaz, Lucy Liu and Drew Barrymore in a film together. I remember thinking, *God, I'd love to do that!*

I did try and learn guitar when I was a wee girl and was pretty pleased with myself when I could play the intro to 'That's Entertainment' by The Jam. Then I learned 'Wonderwall', but to be fair, I think that is possibly the easiest song to play on the guitar ever. And then for a little while after that, I wanted to learn how to play the drums. And when my dad found out about that, the next thing I knew there was a drum kit in the garage. I think he was just pleased that I was showing an interest in music. My brother, Stephen, had a more eclectic music taste. I discovered The Stone Roses through him (my dad really didn't like them), but because I was into the same music that my dad was, I think I ended up providing this sort of flashback to when he was younger. And I can really understand that feeling now, watching my boys Harrison and Jude discover The Beatles and thinking they're the best thing in the world – it really takes me back to when

I did that. You can tell just by talking to Harrison and Jude that The Beatles are a kind of otherworldly, holy presence to them. They've put them on a pedestal. And I remember thinking exactly like that.

Also, people keep telling me that if you've got girls, by the time they get to 15 or 16 they're quite difficult to deal with so I think maybe there was a sense of my dad thinking, *She's not going to be like this for ever – she's going to discover boys and going out*, so he must have felt like he'd got me for a bit. And I did play the drums for a while, but looking back, I think what I needed was a teacher. My parents got me the stuff, but I think there's only so far you can go on your own, unless you're amazingly talented. And obviously I wasn't.

James taught himself and pretty much learned everything he knows by just sitting in his room going over and over the same songs on guitar until he had mastered them. Harrison is definitely the same. You can clearly see his passion is guitar; he plays it morning, noon and night, and luckily for him, it seems to come very naturally. Jude is equally as passionate but, like me, he has to work on it. He has to make an effort to learn (like most people would). Both ways will pay off, but they are playing and learning how to play really differently. Jude has taken up playing the bass so there's never any arguments about who's turn it is on which guitar, which is a relief!

So while I couldn't play the guitar very well, I still wanted to look the part. It started with the parka, then the Lonsdale jumpers, then the target sewn on to the back of every coat I owned. My dad massively encouraged it and kept buying me patches for my parkas. He bought me a bag for school with a picture of a Vespa on it. My mum went along with it, but I think she must have been fed up listening to the same music and sewing patches on to jackets.

My fascination with the mods carried on for some time, so for my seventeenth birthday, rather than the second-hand car that my friends seemed to be getting from their parents, mine bought me a 1982 duck-egg-blue Vespa. Of course, it was my dad's idea and so he and his mate drove all the way to England in a hired van to pick it up for me. I'll never forget stepping outside and seeing it sitting on the driveway, polished to an inch of its life! I couldn't believe it was mine! It was amazing but I could barely ride it because it was way too big and heavy for me, so my dad took me to empty car parks and I'd just basically go around in circles. In hindsight, I probably looked really 'uncool'! I pimped it up with things like The Who's target logo right at the front, the Beatles logo and a sticker of the Small Faces album *The Autumn Stone* (the one with 'Itchycoo Park' on). Because I'm on the shorter side, my mum had always been worried that someone would just come and take it off me when I was stopped at some traffic lights or something. But in the end, I physically couldn't use it so my dad rode it for a little while but then one day he nearly got into what could have been a really bad accident and my mum was like, 'We're done with the scooter guys' and that was that. So we sold it.

Clair's Desert Island Discs

The idea on *Desert Island Discs* is that you can choose eight tracks you'd take with you if you were marooned on a desert island. I tried really hard to mix it up a bit and include different bands. Well, a bit. But The Beatles are a huge part of my life, so much so that our two boys are called Harrison and Jude, which I'll go into later. Both of them are completely obsessed with The Beatles right now. They're not far off the ages that James and I were when we discovered our love of music. Anyway, Harrison had just watched something on YouTube where modern bands were explaining that The Beatles had paved the way for everything and that basically their bands wouldn't even be here if The Beatles hadn't done what they did first. And then James and Harrison got talking about it and James said (kind of joking, but also kind of not joking), 'If The Beatles hadn't existed, your mum and dad might not have got together!' And to be fair, he's right. The Beatles were the first subject that James and I spoke about and the first big thing we had in common. So, in a way, The Beatles did draw us to each other.

I'm not sure I would have been as into music as I am now if I hadn't discovered The Beatles at such a young age. And I certainly wouldn't have gone through my life knowing for sure that if I ever had kids, and the first was a boy, which somehow I knew the baby would be, that he'd be called Harrison. After George. George Harrison was/is probably my most favourite person in the world! I've been in love with him since I was 12 years old, and it was at about that age that I had decided on my child's name. Even if it had been a girl, that baby would have been named after George Harrison.

James was very much into different time periods of music, but I really stuck to the sixties and seventies. I did love Oasis and thought The Libertines were cool (and I was a little in love with Pete Doherty for a while) but bands like The Beatles and The Jam have just been a constant in my life, so they feature a lot in the list.

I'll tell you what I'd actually throw into the waves rather than listen to it if it turned up on my desert island and that's any dance and house music. Even when I was 18 and getting ready to go out, I'd be listening to

The Beatles and it drove my mates mental. They wanted the clubland tunes on, but I couldn't bear it! A couple of years later it became a little more bearable for my friends as I'd switched out The Beatles for Amy Winehouse and The Kooks and they could handle them.

Trying to put eight tracks together for an imaginary *Desert Island Discs* show was an impossible task. If they made you choose eight bands rather than songs, I'd be fine! I probably wouldn't even need the complete eight! But here goes…

'A Day in the Life' by The Beatles

I think I was 11 when I first heard 'A Day in the Life'. I remember being in my room, either on a weekend or a school holiday and being a bit bored, but listening to The Beatles, obviously. I lay down on the bed, looked out the window and just totally forgot where I was and what I was doing. Towards the end of the song, it builds up with a dramatic crescendo. Once it was finished, silent for a few seconds, I thought *Woooah! Holy shit – that was some song!* I know I was young and was just properly discovering all about The Beatles but that was the first song that I just lost myself in. It felt like I'd come out of a trance when it ended.

'Start!' by The Jam

The album *Sound Affects* was one of a bunch of albums by The Jam that my dad gave me to listen to along with *All Mod Cons* and *In the City*. I remember copying The Jam's logo (which was sprayed on to a tiled wall on the album cover for *In the City*) in literally all of my schoolbooks. 'Start!' is my dad's favourite song by The Jam and he told me that early on, so I think it sort of naturally became my favourite too. When you're young and you're introduced to something one of your parents loves, you instantly form a connection to it, you ask them questions about it and the answers you get back you take as gospel. So, if my dad said something like 'Don't listen to this band, they're shit', I'd just repeat exactly that to my friends if someone ever mentioned that band. Although he did that with The Stone Roses and I have to say, he was wrong, of course. But I never listened to them until my older brother told me to, so we disagree on some music stuff.

I do love 'Down in the Tube Station at Midnight' and 'That's Entertainment' but I think I've gone with 'Start!' because it's the one that means the most rather than going for the one song I'd listen to if someone asked me what I fancied putting on the record player. I feel like you should be allowed to choose two lists for *Desert Island Discs* – one for the songs that mean the most to you and one for the songs you want to listen to all the time!

But there's another reason for choosing 'Start!' and that's because I love the song 'Taxman' by The Beatles, so it's kind of a double whammy. But, and James always says he thinks this is crazy, I heard 'Start!' (which was released in 1980) before I heard 'Taxman' (which was on *Revolver*, released in 1966). So, to me, it did feel a bit like The Beatles had been inspired by The Jam rather than the other way around!

'Sha-La-La-La-Lee' by Small Faces

Small Faces were another band that my dad encouraged me towards. He bought me *Ogden's Nut Gone Flake* (their third album and only concept album) and I used to listen to that over and over again. I thought Steve Marriott's voice was unbelievable. But as soon as I heard 'Sha-La-La-La-Lee', which was on their debut album, I just thought, *What a tune*. I played it by myself in my room a lot. It's still one of my favourite songs and I absolutely love it.

'Behind Blue Eyes' by The Who

I'm not completely happy with this choice just because it's so hard to choose one song by The Who. I know it's very cliché, but 'My Generation' is one of the greatest songs of all time. 'The Kids are Alright' is also one of my favourite songs and 'Substitute' might have been the first song by The Who that I really loved so I get very sentimental about that one. 'Substitute' would probably be the song that gets an honourable mention.

But I've gone for 'Behind Blue Eyes' because it takes me back to when James and I were in the car (we'd just started going out together) and I played The Who on my phone and started singing 'Behind Blue Eyes' with everything I had and James just found it hilarious, so I'll always remember it for that silly moment. But it's also one of my favourite songs by The Who.

I actually saw The Who (well, half of The Who) at T in the Park in 2006 and that was an amazing festival. They were headlining on the Sunday and Paul Weller was on the night before. Arctic Monkeys were also playing on the Saturday and The Kooks played on the Sunday as well, who I still love, so it was a pretty decent line-up to say the least. The Kooks' record *Inside In/Inside Out* had just come out and it's a staple album. I still listen to it and it's one of those rare albums where you don't have to skip any song!

I was 18 when I went to that festival and I remember thinking when I was waiting for The Who to come on stage, *I can't believe this is actually happening*. When I first started listening to their music, I never thought I'd actually get to see them. I'd just finished sixth year (I think this is called sixth form in England) where I had sat my advanced higher in Art and Drama, and I and went to the festival with my best friend Kashka. There were some other people we knew going as well and my big brother Stephen (four years older than me) was also going along with some of his friends. Our mum had been going on about us sticking together, seeing as it was the first time that I'd been to a festival and I was only 18, so Stephen (who'd been to T in the Park a few times already) told me he'd camp 'near us' – i.e. close enough that if I needed him, he'd be there, but not right next to us. My mum started putting together a 'bag of essentials' for me – face wipes and my own toilet roll, a little deodorant and all that sort of stuff, which was nice, but all I was concerned about was how we were going to get a load of cheap alcohol in so we wouldn't have to pay a fortune for it there.

Back in the day, Stephen was very well known for partying (he's not like this now!) and when I first started to venture out into the pubs and clubs I was just known as Stephen's wee sister. My brother joined the RAF and ended up touring Afghanistan a couple of times. That brought us a lot closer, because I missed him and worried about him. So, when he came back, we both seemed to have grown up and there wasn't really any brother–sister fighting or bickering after that. In fact, we got on really well. We're still quite close now but not in an obvious way. It's the kind of relation-ship where we don't talk that much but if something happened, I'd be right there for him and vice versa. (To be honest, I've got a lot of friends I'd say I was close to, but I don't talk to any of them regularly either!) Myself, James and the kids are close to my brother and his wife Louise and my little niece and nephew, Callan and Brodie, and we try to spend a lot of time together when we can – they come here for half-term holidays, over the summer holidays and the kids have all been to Legoland and Disneyland Paris together, that sort of thing. Stephen's birthday, his son's and my Harrison's are all within three days of each other, so we always get together and do something around then.

I didn't go to T in the Park again, because I uprooted and moved down to London from Scotland soon after the festival ended, but I'll never forget it and that moment The Who took the stage was epic.

'The Girl in the Dirty Shirt' by Oasis

I've gone back and forth on this one because I grew up listening to Oasis but I found it difficult narrowing it down. And this is another case of struggling to get the balance right between songs you want to listen to and songs that really mean something to you because you remember listening to them during important parts of your life. 'The Girl in the Dirty Shirt' falls into the 'soppy reason for including it' category. Part of the reason is because it came along at a time when I was old enough to go out and buy the CD, which felt really cool. And another part is because I think I was in love with Liam for a bit, but the main reason is because 'The Girl in the Dirty Shirt' would be on VH1 and MTV a lot on the telly in the living room when I was at my gran and papa's house. Whenever it came on the TV, my grandad, who I call papa, would say, 'Oh, there's Clair's song on again!' In fairness, I was a bit of a tomboy (and possibly a bit grubby), but when he first heard the lyrics, he said, 'This is you, Clair!' and I've never forgotten that. But if I was actually stuck on a desert island, I probably wouldn't listen to it because it would just make me sad, thinking of my papa. Actually, come to think of it, I'm not sure I'd want any music on my desert island because it would just depress me, remembering better times!

'You Really Got Me' by The Kinks

The Kinks were another band that my dad introduced me to. 'You Really Got Me' is such an iconic song and even if you're not a big music fan, you'll recognize the tune even if you don't know who it's by. But it was between this, 'Itchycoo Park', 'All Day and All of the Night', 'Dedicated Follower of Fashion' and 'Sunny Afternoon'. What a few songs they are! But I just thought, *I could listen to 'You Really Got Me' over and over again*, so it makes the list.

When I was growing up in a family of four, we never went on long car journeys, so we didn't have that situation James did when his dad would stick something in the cassette player and that's what you'd listen to on the way. But then my little sister Rebecca came along ten years after me and my mum and dad found a new lease of life, so the three of them went on holidays together. (I was seventeen and Stephen was twenty-one at that point, doing our own things.) But that worked out for me and Stephen because that meant house parties! I don't think my parents know how many we had, but they definitely know about one that Stephen had. (Although I was there with a couple of friends, I'd just been dumped and remember being a bit annoyed he was having a party because I just wanted to sit on the couch, wallowing and watching telly.) My parents had a built-in hot tub in the garden and a little while after they came back from holiday, my mum opened it up and found a couple of things floating in there that definitely shouldn't have been (that's all I'm saying), and they didn't belong to me or my brother, but they were furious.

'Ticket to Ride' by The Beatles

This was my favourite Beatles song for years so this had to go on my list. One of the best things about it to me was that it's all 'She's got a ticket to ride / But she don't care' so I could put myself in *her* shoes. It all fed into my Wednesday Addams vibe that I had going on. I knew how incredibly cool I was, but everybody else my age thought I was insanely uncool. And I remember saying, 'You guys will realize how cool I am eventually…one day!'

'Something' by The Beatles

I love George Harrison more than I could ever explain. I don't use this word a lot in my life but it's a *beautiful* song. It's a very personal song for George, written about his first wife Pattie, and is one of the best love songs ever written in my opinion.

When I was first introduced to The Beatles, I wanted to learn more about them. So I went on the PC at home (back when you'd only have one device in the place that connected to the Internet and you took it in turns on it) and dug a bit deeper. I won't lie – I did think George was the cutest thing I'd ever seen, so I had a huge crush on him. But, when I first discovered The Beatles, my dad gave me a copy of *A Hard Day's Night* (the film) and told me, 'This is them – you actually get to see them, walking and talking.' And that blew my mind. Right in the opening scene, the four boys are running from a bunch of scream-ing fans down a street and George trips. And it wasn't like he was tripping comically for the movie, he prop-erly goes down and to be honest, that was it, that was when my love affair began and it just got more and more intense. And this was a pretty big deal as a 14-year-old girl because I started thinking, *I'm never going to fall in love with anyone else, because no one's going to live up to George Harrison, so I'm fu**ed and I'll never be happy!* And I know that all sounds ridiculous now but that is genu-inely how I felt at the time. And to a certain extent, I'm still devastated that I never got my chance!

Back in the mid-2000s, I got a tattoo which is just 'The Beatles' written in their iconic font. It was on my stomach, so you could see it when I was wearing low-rise jeans and a crop top. But after having two babies it was all stretched out and looked really terrible so I ended up having it covered up. It would have been so much cooler if I'd put a little bit more thought into it rather than just getting the name of the band. I was insanely proud of it back then and used it kind of like a way to prove to people how much of a Beatles fan I really was. But it wasn't exactly the kind of tattoo you might expect someone aged 18 to go for. It was kind of rebellious and not rebellious at the same time.

I didn't tell my mum and dad about the tattoo. I figured I could just hide it when they were around. But shortly after I'd had it done, my mum came in my room and I'd left the dressing on my desk. It was covered in ink and blood. She asked me if I had a tattoo (she was aware of what a tattoo dressing looked like, as my dad has loads of tats) and stumped, I said yes but told her it was only a henna one that would last a couple of weeks. She was a little unconvinced, but when she asked my dad about it, he explained henna tattoos would not need a dressing and there certainly wouldn't be any blood, so I was rumbled! I thought I was going to get in trouble, but apparently my dad just said, 'Well at least it's something cool.' It was a pretty ridiculous thing for an 18-year-old to get done, but you can't exactly get mad for someone getting a Beatles tattoo, can you? Especially when it was your dad who helped start this whole obsession!

'Are You Lonesome Tonight' by Elvis Presley

This was actually a late addition because somehow I'd forgotten how much I love Elvis when working on this list, but this one genuinely gives me goosebumps. Elvis has his cool rock 'n' roll-y voice for most of this song, but there are a few points where he really belts out a note in this sort of Frank Sinatra style. And every time he does that, my hairs stand up on the back of my neck. And not that he comes anywhere close to George, but Elvis is so gorgeous as well. Just a side note.

'Go Your Own Way' by Fleetwood Mac

Fleetwood Mac are one of my favourite bands. Stevie Nicks is a goddess, the coolest chick ever, in my opinion, so they had to be in somewhere. But which song do you go for when you've got so many classics to choose from, like 'The Chain', 'I Don't Want to Know' and 'Dreams'?

I've gone for 'Go Your Own Way' and part of the reason for that is because it reminds me of being in our current house. When we moved in here, we brought three record players with us and put them in different rooms. We both brought our separate record collections with us and then we started ordering albums that we knew we had to have in the house. We always wanted to have music playing when the kids were growing up. Fleetwood Mac reminds me of being a grown-up, having my own record player in my house and playing it on a Saturday when I'd be doing boring jobs around the house like cleaning the floors. And I imagine the kids saying when they're older that they remember this song because it reminds them of their mum doing the house-work. I don't think my dad was a big Fleetwood Mac fan because I don't remember any of their albums being on when we were growing up. And I don't really remember listening to them with James either. So, this one's just for me. It felt like something I properly discovered when I became a mum, belting it out when I'm doing house-work. *Rumours* is one of the best albums of all time, in my opinion. We're talking in the top five albums of all time kind of territory. It's hit after hit.

I will say that putting together just eight desert island discs has been painful. And I'm going to break the rules and mention a few more which are really important to me. 'A Hard Day's Night' was the first Beatles song and first Beatles album I heard. And 'I Feel Fine' is up there too. Harrison was playing his guitar recently and just made that same feedback sound that they left in at the beginning of 'I Feel Fine' and he stopped, looked at me and said, 'What do you think that is?' And I said, 'I know what it is, it's "I Feel Fine"!' And he went, 'Yeah! Did you know that that was a mistake and they stuck that in—' So I had to cut in and say, 'Let me just stop you there, son. No, no, no, no, no, no – you don't get to school Mum on The Beatles!'

To be fair to him, he has actually told me a couple of things I didn't know and it is a good laugh seeing him try to out-Beatles me. And any time he does, he's so pleased, pumping his little fist. He's mad into them and to be honest, James and I kind of had that coming. I named him after George Harrison for one! But how horrendous would it be if either of them hated The Beatles?! And I know sometimes that does happen when kids are exposed to something you love so much and they rebel against it or just genuinely don't like it. Let's hope that if it does happen, it'll just be a phase, but I think they're already too far gone now. Harrison's obsessed with playing the guitar, keeps talking about how he's going to be in a band and thinks he's going to be the next John Lennon. So, I think we're safe on the everyone liking The Beatles front. Although I have found myself saying things to Harrison like, 'Just in case you don't become the world's next John Lennon, you know who else is really cool? Scientists and doctors!'

My mum and dad met through my mum's friend Carol. She and my mum were best friends from a young age. Carol said to my mum one day, 'I think you'd like my big cousin David.' And to be fair, she was right, because they ended up getting married! Carol, who's always been Aunt Carol to me, moved to Los Angeles when I was about three, but we have always made lots of visits over there to see her and her family. Carol's dad, my father's Uncle Davie, died about 20 years ago and so Carol's mum, Dora, went to LA to live with her. My dad and his Aunt Dora are very close, so it's great when we all go over there.

When I was ten, my aunt, my cousin and I flew to Florida for a holiday. We went to SeaWorld, which absolutely blew my mind and I became completely obsessed with killer whales, and we're talking nearly Beatles level of obsession. I'd never seen anything like it when I saw them up close. I started talking about wanting to become a SeaWorld trainer and moving to Florida. When I got older, I learned more and more about SeaWorld and similar places and realized that they weren't doing things that I loved at all when it came to animal welfare. Then the film *The Cove* came out, which followed former dolphin trainer Ric O'Barry filming dolphin-hunting practices in Japan.

In the 1960s, Ric O'Barry actually trained the five dolphins used to play Flipper on the US TV show. He had one of the dolphins, called Kathy, in his care for years in a specialized enclosure attached to a beach house that the TV network paid for and Ric treated her as his friend. But Kathy became more lethargic over time and one day she went under the water but didn't come up for air. Ric swears that she deliberately drowned herself because she was completely healthy so there was no other possible explanation. She just didn't want to display and perform any more. So, he quit his job and became an activist. He is trying to educate the world on these big parks: they are fooling visitors into thinking that they're learning about the animals, but in reality, they're learning as much from a whale in a tank as they would do about humans if they visited a prisoner on death row. You're not actually learning anything about how an animal lives or normally behaves. In 1970, Ric founded the Dolphin Project, which is dedicated to the welfare and protection of dolphins.

This whole story really affected me and I became really passionate about it the more I read. And now, every Christmas as my main present James makes a donation to the Dolphin Project. The first couple of times I posted it on to my social media and Ric has got in touch a few times after seeing those posts. One of these times when I'm visiting my family, I still have a plan to drive down to SeaWorld in San Diego from Los Angeles and protest outside the entrance. It doesn't have to be a big organized thing, but if I can change one person's mind when they're in the queue to get into SeaWorld, that'll be something. I've seen protestors have that effect on people and it's an amazing, inspiring thing. If people keep paying to go to SeaWorld, the whole practice is never going to end. And if no one went, SeaWorld would have no reason to keep these amazing animals captive. So that's my dream. Maybe we'll shoot it for a vlog one day!

Soon after I met James, he came over to LA with me, and my family out there fell in love with him. When you land in LA and you're driving and you've got palm trees and the sun and you see places like Wendy's restaurant with their huge billboards, you can't help but get excited. It's an exciting place to be. James would go there tomorrow, though, and he still loves to go out there for pilot season when he can (the time when production studios and TV networks cast and make sample shows which may, or may not, get picked up for a whole series). Carol, her husband Scot and my great Aunt Dora are always happy to have him, so he stays in their spare room, which is now basically James's room.

The rest of my family are in Scotland, though. And my grandad, who I call my papa, and I were very close. He passed away in 2008, just before I met James. And that really annoys me because my papa would have been so happy to meet him and see that I was being taken care of.

I spent a lot of time with my gran and papa through my childhood, as did my siblings and cousins. We have quite a large family and my happiest childhood memories are of Saturday nights spent at my gran and papa's house. My gran would be in the kitchen making a big dinner for everyone (which was my parents, three aunties and their husbands and all their respective children), we'd eat and watch Saturday night telly: *Blind Date*, *The Generation*

Game. It was a really happy time. Every day after school, all my cousins and I would head back from school to gran and papa's house, CBBC would go on and you'd wait for dinner – the usual stuff of mince and tatties, or in the hotter months a plate of salad with boiled eggs, slices of packet ham and some chips. The days spent there and the upbringing from my gran and papa, with their old-fashioned values, really set me and all the kids on the paths we are on today. We all have the same values of family and keeping down-to-earth no matter where you are or what you do.

James: As a kid, I was obsessed with films and TV. From secondary school I knew that I wanted to do something telly related but I never actually thought it would be a career. And I certainly didn't think it was something that would actually make me money. I'm not from a showbiz background by any means so I didn't really have any idea what I was doing, but I just kind of took every opportunity I could, kept turning up everywhere and kept saying yes to things! While my mates were having a bit of fun at the weekend, playing football and messing around, I was at acting and singing classes.

Not Glad It's All Over: FA Cup Final 2016

I've been a Crystal Palace fan since I was tiny, but I moved from Croydon to Dagenham when I was two, so all my mates are West Ham fans. The first football match I went to was a pre-season game against Spurs at Selhurst Park. I must have been seven or eight and my dad and my uncle took me. That day I was introduced to the unique pain of being a football fan. The agony and the ecstasy. Although, that's probably more accurately 75 per cent agony and 25 per cent ecstasy.

I'll start with the highs. The 1997 First Division play-off final was the best game I'd seen up until that point, with David Hopkin scoring an absolute stunner from 25 yards with almost the last kick of the game. In 2011 there was Darren Ambrose's wonder strike from about 35 yards against Man United in the League Cup at Old Trafford which took us into the semi-final. I was actually supposed to go to that game, but I'm glad I didn't because that goal definitely wouldn't have happened if I had been there. And then there was Kevin Phillips coming on and scoring the penalty that took us to the Premier League in the 2013 Championship play-off final against Watford. I felt sick with nerves for the whole game until that penalty.

The biggest low was probably losing the 2016 FA Cup final, which I watched at the local social club in Dagenham, a place I'd been drinking at since I was 18. It's a West Ham pub and some might say it was an odd venue to watch Palace play Man United in the cup final, especially because if Palace won the match, West Ham wouldn't qualify into the Europa League for the next season. So, there were quite a few West Ham fans there who really didn't want Palace to win. But, at that time it was pretty much my second home so they just about let me get away with it.

I was with my friend Jalaal Hartley and we were recording an episode of our podcast *Dream Team FC*, which we'd started back in 2015. You can hear Clair in the background and she's obviously massively interested in the game because you can hear her talking about The Beatles.

So just to give you a bit of background (and to build up the tension): Man United hadn't reached the FA Cup final since 2007 (they lost to Chelsea that year) but Palace had last been to Wembley in 1990 when we lost to Man United after a replay (yup, that used to happen) because the first match ended in a 3–3 draw.

I can't remember ever wanting to win a game so much. And it looked like it might happen too when we had the ball in the back of the net after 17 minutes. I still get annoyed about this now. Connor Wickham is on the break and gets brought down by Chris Smalling, but Wickham gets up and scores past David De Gea only for referee Mark Clattenburg to insist on awarding the free kick rather than play the advantage. I had a few words to say on the podcast.

And then, at 78 minutes, Jason Puncheon, who'd been my hero all season, scored and everything changed. The only time I can remember feeling that way was when I watched Dagenham & Redbridge (who were then a non-league team playing in the Vauxhall Conference) beat Exeter City (then in the Third Division) 3–0 in an FA Cup second-round replay at Victoria Road in 2001 with some of my mates. It was a giant killing, a cupset if you will. I was right at the front and when the final whistle blew, I saw everyone jumping over the advertising hoardings, so I joined in...only, none of my mates followed me! So I ran from one end of the pitch to the other and jumped up and over the hoardings on the other side, and didn't stay on the pitch to celebrate along with anyone else. Running directly to the other side of the pitch was also the quickest way out of the ground, so I beat the crowd leaving, and as any football fan can appreciate, there's something really satisfying about a quick stadium exit!

Anyway, back to the Palace goal. My phone blew up. Alan Pardew did a little dance. Everything was amazing. But then, with 12 minutes to hold on for, I started feeling sick and really hot as Man United threw everything at us. But I didn't have to feel sick for that long because Juan Mata scored 3 minutes later. Also, outrageously, someone other than me farted, which added insult to injury. It stank and I knew it was someone close, my mate Chris eventually owned up. When I think about that fart, I sometimes understand how Clair feels when I do a bad one.

The game went on to extra time, then just before the break Chris Smalling got sent off for a second bookable offence. Was this our chance? No, because Man United scored again and won. I felt like I was paying the price for the high of Palace winning the Championship play-off final in 2013.

And it's sort of what I expected and I tried so hard to prepare myself emotionally for this outcome. It makes sense. It's correct in the universe that Manchester United should beat Crystal Palace I guess, but it doesn't make losing an FA Cup final easy. It's a horrible feeling that I know I've shared with millions of others. Man United didn't play badly, Crystal Palace weren't embarrassing, didn't shrink at the challenge, made their fans proud and tried their hardest. It's what football's about. There were even tears running down my non-football fan friend Jalaal's cheeks.

When I was about eight years old, I started going to a local stage school. It all started when one of my primary school teachers, Mrs Lovett (you always remember the name of your favourite teacher, don't you?), thought I had quite a good singing voice and said I should have proper lessons. And so my mum and dad found somewhere local, but it was a stage school, so they did the whole lot: singing, dancing and acting. I joined the Saturday stage school for singing lessons in the morning, and I went to a normal school during the week. All the other kids at the stage school were there all week though.

I didn't have any mates at primary school who were doing similar things, but I was a bit of a joker at school and so acting and singing kind of went with my personality, I think. I remember one time me and some of the other kids from the stage school did a performance at Romford market and part of it was a dance routine (the full jazz hands and everything), which I was a bit crap at, but I got involved as much as I could. A bunch of my mates from school came to watch it and let's just say that was a tough one to live down. It got brought up for years to come.

I remember auditioning for a production that the stage school were putting on, and after that, the people who ran the school suggested that I join them full-time. They told my parents not to worry about the extra cost – one singing lesson had already been a stretch – and they'd look after me. Little helping hands like that have been extended at quite a few points in my career. I've genuinely been really lucky and wouldn't be where I am today without people like Mrs Lovett, and Kathy Blackburn at the stage school. And the stage school wasn't making Kathy any money by any means – she just enjoyed seeing kids with potential and trying to help them. I was a nice kid, I wasn't particularly annoying or anything like that. Well, when I was out of the house at least! People didn't seem to mind helping me out and they seemed to see something in me that they thought was worth developing. I think about that sort of stuff all the time, because things could have been wildly different if it wasn't for those people who showed up at what turned out to be massively important moments in my life. After working with Kathy Blackburn, I went to Colin's Performing Arts in Romford, which was run, funnily enough, by a bloke called Colin.

My mum and dad bought me some tap shoes, not that I was any good at tap. They were really nice ones and cost them a bit of money. But after about a year of them sitting in the box, Colin kept telling me I was wasting those tap shoes, so I ended up giving them to him. He bloody loved them and was still wearing them years after I'd left. They still had my name in biro on the sole! It was good to see them being put to good use though.

Whistle Down the Wind was my first professional job around Christmas 1998 and I had to get permission from my school to do it because I had to take quite a lot of time off. I was 11 years old and it was actually the first audition I'd ever done, going for the part of Clarence. And then, I got it, and suddenly found myself in the cast of a West End show! It was performing at the Aldwych Theatre just off the Strand. I'd grown up watching musicals like *Grease, Oliver!* and *The Lion King*, so this was a dream come true.

One of my castmates was Jessica Cornish, who became Jessie J a bit later down the line. The cast had about 12 kids in it and we all had little solo sections in some of the numbers. I was in the second load of kids to join the original cast, because I think when you were under 16 you could only work on a production for six months so they'd change the children's cast quite regularly. To coincide with the PR offensive when the musical launched in the West End (it got a lot of press because the music was composed by Andrew Lloyd Webber and the lyricist was Jim Steinman, famous for all sorts of pop hits including 'Total Eclipse of the Heart' and 'I'd Do Anything For Love (But I Won't Do That)'), Boyzone recorded a cover of 'No Matter What', the number that we sang at the end of act one. That went on to be a massive hit.

There were two teams of kids in the children's cast and we'd have one week on, one week off, with nine performances a week (one every evening plus matinees on two days). We had chaperones, so two adults were looking after about a dozen of us and they'd take you out for lunch and dinner. The funny thing was, I used to travel from home to the theatre by myself each day, jumping on the Tube from Dagenham Heathway, getting off at Temple and walking up towards the Strand. I'd got used to that kind of thing though. I'd grown up quickly and loved working with the cast. It was a great show to be a part of and I had a lot of fun doing it.

So, after the six-month break that you had to take after you'd been working on a show for six months, I went straight into another audition, this time for *Les Misérables* at the Palace Theatre, located where Shaftesbury Avenue meets Charing Cross Road. And to my surprise, I got it. I'd been to two auditions and got two jobs and it was then that I started thinking I might not be bad at this acting thing! Again, I had to get permission from my school to do it, but I think they understood that this was something I really wanted to do and to be honest, was probably a better use of everyone's time.

Being in a show at the Palace Theatre was a massive deal for me then. I think it's still the best theatre in London. Most of the other theatres in the West End are just kind of on the streets, they've got some awnings and stuff outside them, but the Palace is a massive building stood by itself in Cambridge Circus. I remember thinking that if I could be in a show at any theatre, it would be that one. It's got that area in front of it where everyone's milling about, it's got the big display out the front and everyone knows where it is. There's a bit of theatre to the theatre and it was a big show with pretty much a full house every night. And on top of that, Gavroche was a great part. He's the little street urchin who knows all the comings and goings. He does a lot of storytelling, pushing the tale along, having that direct effect on which way everything goes, running up and down the barricades and then a heroic death. And seeing as *Oliver!* wasn't on in the West End back then, Gavroche was probably one of the best parts around for someone my age. I remember thinking that if I could do this for the rest of my life, I'd take it. I got on so well with the cast, everyone was so nice to me and Hal Fowler, who played Javert, had a lot of time for me, encouraging me and sharing jokes.

This is going to sound a bit tragic, but I think I had a look about me where people felt sorry for me. I would get stuff for free and it became a kind of theme of my childhood. When my mum took me to see *Oliver!* when I was much younger, she went to the toilet and told me to wait next to the kiosk for her. When she came back, I'd got a hat, a neckerchief, some crisps and chocolate. And she was like, 'Where did you get all this stuff from?' And I said, 'They just started talking to me and gave it to me.' But this sort of thing happened all the time. People seemed to be worried about me. Maybe I just looked fragile. But I was streetwise, a bit like Gavroche. I could sense dodgy people and potential problem situations and steered well clear.

★

I moved from Croydon to Dagenham when I was two and growing up there was a different world to what it is now. I was playing in bomb shelters, people were still talking about the Germans and we used to hang out in a bombed-out hospital that was still standing over the field behind my primary school. Across the road from the primary school was the Ford factory and the mentality that was fed to me growing up was that if you kept your nut down, did well and worked hard, there might be a job for you across the road. And then eventually maybe a company car and a mortgage on a house.

My nan was 41 when my mum was born so she'd lived through the war, working in a munitions factory in London when she was 21. So I always felt like I'd grown up with a connection to that wartime generation. My mum worked for the Home Office in Queen Anne's Gate in Westminster from when she was about 16 until around 2010 and now she works for the local council. My dad was a painter and decorator – that was the family trade, which my dad, his brother Steve and my grandad Paddy all did. And then I was born and when I was about five or six, my mum wanted him to get a job that wasn't cash in hand so he ended up working for Parcelforce around Lakeside and then went on to become a postman for Royal Mail.

We weren't rich growing up but I only really realized that when I was a lot older. I remember one time I made my mum feel really guilty because I wanted a toy and it was like £5 from the Argos catalogue. It wasn't my birthday or

Christmas or anything but I just really wanted it. And she went out and got it for me. I've never forgotten that because that will have meant that something they needed to pay for that week didn't end up getting paid.

I am very proud of where I'm from and I'm proud of where I am now, but don't get me wrong, my life has been the result of a series of lucky breaks, and I really do believe that. I've got friends that I went to stage school with who were, and are, a lot more talented than me, who haven't had the luck that I've had. But so much of acting success depends on being in the right place at the right time. And that sort of thing has happened to me, maybe a dozen times. You could be the best actor in the world, but things still have to align for you to get put up for that particular part, meet that particular casting director or end up performing in something that for whatever reason in that precise moment in time does something to capture the public imagination. And until then, you're going for acting jobs here and there, doing your best and hoping that something comes of it. And along the way you get to meet people your age that are doing the same thing, auditioning for the same parts or similar parts in things. Adverts, especially when you're early on in your career, can be a lifesaver for actors because they're a couple of days' work and they'll fund you for a good while.

One of those people who was up for the same sort of roles as me at the same time was Hannah Tointon. I met her on a Doritos advert in Amsterdam in about 2004, although it wasn't my first advert. That honour went to

Hellmann's, where I played a little squirt advising a burger salesman on what sauce he should stick on his burgers. (We actually spoke about this on the vlog, as we worked with Hellmann's again as a sponsor for an episode of *At Home With The Buckleys*.) They tweaked my voice though, so it sounded like I'd just inhaled a whole helium balloon. Anyway, back to Doritos, who were giving away virtual pets, and that was the theme of the advert. Hannah and I were boyfriend and girlfriend (in the advert) and I get introduced to her parents as her new boyfriend. And as I'm munching on a bowl of Doritos, Hannah announces to her parents that she and I are having a baby (the joke being it's really a virtual pet).

By then I was quite used to travelling to places by myself, although that was the first time I'd gone abroad for a job. The ad took three or four days to film and I literally ate cheese-flavoured Doritos all day every day for the whole time. Honestly, it was probably five or six years before I had cheese Doritos again and that was just about enough time to cleanse the palate. I remember wandering into the red light district (by accident, of course) with Hannah and the couple who played her parents and we didn't know where to look. There were just naked women standing in bright windows and I remember being really embarrassed and going really red, not that anyone could see that. I remember standing in the doorway of one of the coffee shops – that's as far as I got in. Whenever there was a cool or weird situation, I didn't know how to handle it and got embarrassed.

★

One of the first big steps you take as a young actor is getting a featured part in a classic long-running drama like *The Bill*. So many actors have started this way, like Sean Bean, Mark Strong, Keira Knightley, Idris Elba, James McAvoy and David Tennant. I was in *The Bill* three times in three years (playing different characters). It was a great place to get experience, understand how things work on a set and how everyone does their jobs. I had a great time on *The Bill*. I did an episode with Gary Lucy, which was a lot of fun. And if you enjoy it, you start thinking, *OK, I'm going to try and carry on with this*, but it's not for everyone, and some people come away and think, *This was horrible* and don't pursue acting any further. But I loved it.

2

 **James**: In 2006, when I was 18, I got a call from my agent. A couple of guys had written a pilot called *Baggy Trousers* about a bunch of kids at school, which I auditioned for and got the role of Neil. It was set in the 1980s when the writers – Damon Beesley and Iain Morris – were growing up. They were producers on Channel 4's *The 11 O'Clock Show* (which was the first time that most of us had seen Sacha Baron Cohen and Ricky Gervais among others) and formed their own production company a few years later.

After we shot the pilot, I didn't hear back about it for over a year, so I kind of presumed nothing more would come of it. And then one day, out of the blue, my agent called me up and said, 'I've got some good news and some bad news about *Baggy Trousers*. The good news is that they're going ahead with the pilot and making a series. The bad news is that they're recasting and you're not going to be in it.' I can't remember the rest of the conversation but recall thinking to myself after she'd gone, *What the hell was the good news then?!*

After a few days, I sent Damon Beesley a text to say that I was happy that the show was going ahead and that

I was really pleased for them. I also said I was gutted that the decision had been made to recast but if there were any parts for an episode that I could do, to let me know because I'd love to be included in it. And then a few minutes later he texted me back saying: 'We want you to come in and read for Jay, did your agent not tell you that?' There must have been crossed wires somewhere, but thank God I sent that text!

So, I ended up reading for Jay with loads of other people playing the three other parts. There were one or two other people reading for Jay as well, but I didn't know that Damon and Iain had basically already chosen me, in their minds at least. They'd rewritten big parts of the original pilot script and the setting had changed. I think the channel wanted something a bit more cool and contemporary to attract an audience in their teens and twenties. And a new name, but this took a while. The producer came up with 'One, Two, Three, Four', which I don't need to say much more about. Another one was 'The Dickheads', which we all quite liked! 'Legends' was another that was spinning around for a bit. Then 'Desperados'. And then someone came up with *The Inbetweeners*, which the four of us all hated to begin with.

On the last audition there were two Neils, two Simons and two Wills but I was the only one reading Jay. We did one read-through and then they brought in Blake Harrison, Joe Thomas and Simon Bird. And we all read through the script together and everything made sense. It was really different reading with them and even in the audition having only just met, we were taking the piss out of each other and making each other laugh. Iain took a picture of the four of us against the white wall behind us and he said that was the moment that he knew he'd found 'the Inbetweeners'. I think it was because we just looked so weird and the photo made him laugh, and to be honest, that's ultimately what you want.

I was the only one of the four guys from the pilot to make it to *The Inbetweeners*. The guy who played Jay in the pilot (the character was actually called Lee then) was Darcy Thomas. He's a really funny bloke and everyone loved him, so Iain and Damon featured him in a few episodes (he's in the first episode taking the piss out of Will when he's wearing his badge and carrying his briefcase) and sometimes I think we'd just find excuses to have him come in and do stuff! The guy who played Simon was Adam, who went off to university. The original Will was Matt Green, who was already a very funny stand-up comedian by that point. He was about 28 at the time, but in fairness, he really didn't look it.

As is the case with most actors, when Joe, Simon, Blake and I were cast on *The Inbetweeners* we were all working either full-time or part-time in completely different other jobs. I was working as a kitchen fitter and I found myself spending most of my time driving to and from Howdens in Lakeside for various clients in the area who were having new kitchens put in. I had a trade card at Howdens, which I've still got somewhere. I remember picking up a kitchen from there one day and someone said, 'Aren't you that bloke off the telly?' And I said 'Yup'. And he replied, 'What you doing here then?' And I said, 'Er, picking up a kitchen.'

Joe (Simon) was working as a private tutor, so he'd help your kid with their maths homework. Blake (Neil) was working in the Chamber of Horrors at Madame Tussauds between the first and second series of *The Inbetweeners*. I don't think he ever got recognized because it was dark in there and I assume he was made up to look like some sort of ghoul. And as for Simon (Will), I don't think he's ever had a proper job in his life!

I remember the first day I went into work on *The Inbetweeners*. There wasn't a studio – it was all done on location. It was only for the third series of the show that we had a set – they built the sixth form common room in a massive PE hall in a disused army barracks. But for the first two series we were always on location. Nothing was built for the show, so the houses you see are just people's houses! We shot all the Rudge Park School scenes at Ruislip High School in west London, which had literally just been built, so I think only Years 7 and 8 were actually in school when we were filming it. The rest of it hadn't opened yet so it was the perfect place for us to shoot a TV show. Things changed when we were making series three, though, because the school was full. And it just wouldn't have been possible to shoot a TV show in front of the students because a lot of the kids at school would have been watching the show.

The first scene I remember shooting (the working title was still *Baggy Trousers* then) was Simon (Will) and Joe (Simon) trying on ridiculous tuxedos for the Christmas ball ('Xmas Party', episode 6). Will keeps banging on about being the chairman of the ball committee and the manager of the shop keeps asking if the suits are 'too jazzy'. The next day we were at Thorpe Park, which was for episode 3 and we were there for a couple of days in the end. Everything was brand new and I'd never really been on set (regularly anyway) before then. On *The Bill* and *Teachers* (I appeared in two episodes in 2004) and for the ads I'd been cast in, I'd just gone in for a day each time (except for the Doritos ad). It was new to all of us and we didn't have a clue what we were doing. I was 19 when we shot that first series and looking back, what we didn't understand is that we weren't just there to have a laugh. It didn't feel like we were making a TV show. It felt like I was spending a lot of time pissing about with my mates, which I loved. Although one thing I didn't like at all was watching myself act, especially the first stuff we filmed. Sometimes it still makes me feel a bit sick. In fact, I still haven't seen the whole of series two of *The Inbetweeners*. But also, I was there when we shot it, going through things loads of times and doing multiple takes for everything, so the idea of me rewatching the show is a bit like watching a video of my day at work! But when I'm not in a scene, I like watching those bits with the other boys acting because they're brilliant.

When we were shooting *The Inbetweeners*, I think subconsciously people thought we were kids; one, because we behaved like them and two, because we looked like kids. I mean we're all wearing school uniforms and we're all (fairly) fresh-faced. I was the youngest, though, of the four of us. Blake was 21, Simon was 22, Joe was 23 and I was 19, but people just forgot that we were actually adults. And to be fair, you wouldn't have guessed.

I think I realized this the most when we started making the second series because we got told we'd been nominated for Best New British TV Comedy at the British Comedy Awards in 2008. That was such a big deal to me. I'd grown up watching the ceremony each year with Jonathan Ross presenting it, and I've been obsessed with British comedy since I could remember. I'll never forget that moment, thinking, *Shit! We're actually going to be at the awards*, but I still don't think it actually sunk in! It was a life-changing moment. So we went to the awards do and I spent £100 on a suit – I'd never needed one before. And we won the award!

The cast of *Skins* were there and that was a big hit of a show that had started over a year before *The Inbetweeners*. It covered similar ground, in that it was about teenagers at sixth form, so the two shows were associated with each other for quite a while. People used to say '*Skins* was how you wanted your life to be as a teenager, but *The Inbetweeners* was actually what it was like.' And that always made me laugh because it's definitely true. *Skins* was all sex, drugs, parties and beautiful people and *The Inbetweeners* was all about failing to have sex, failing to get drugs, failing to get into parties and failing to talk to beautiful people.

James's Tom Collins Cocktail

This is a really simple one to whack together and, to be honest, it's probably my favourite cocktail. If you like cloudy lemonade, you'll love it. Think of it as an alcoholic Fanta Lemon. Plus, Clair likes it too. You just need some sugar syrup, gin, lemon juice and a bit of soda water. And some ice. And that's it. So get it dahn yer.

Take a highball glass and add a little shot of sugar syrup (I buy the fancy Monin stuff rather than making my own).

Add a double shot of gin (you choose the brand – treat yourself).

Add a double shot of lemon juice (I've usually got some Jif in the fridge somewhere).

Top it up with soda water and give it a little stir.

Clair: You know what, it's actually pretty good, this, on a summer's day. I gotta hand it to James. It is refreshing. If only he'd learn to clean up after himself, then I'd really like it when he made me one.

I couldn't really think about the fact that the show had been recognized by critics and awards committees. And to be honest, I've always avoided that sort of thing because on the couple of occasions I have taken myself out of the context of the situation, you go a bit mental. Just starting to process the fact that you're stood there in front of thousands of people with Kylie Minogue kissing you on the cheek and giving you an award is enough to send you loopy. You start wondering, *How the hell have I ended up here?* I remember having that feeling when I got a Christmas card from David Walliams. I thought to myself, *Why is the genius from* Rock Profile *and* Little Britain *sending my family a Christmas card? How did everything get to this point?* So I've found the healthiest thing to do, in terms of my own sanity, is to kind of dissociate yourself from everything, so you're just sort of seeing everything happening and thinking to yourself, *Oh, look, it's Kylie Minogue, that's good isn't it?* It almost feels like going to a zoo for the first time and thinking, *Wow, that's an actual lion.* That's what it felt like to me to see people like Russell Brand, Craig Charles, Matt Lucas, Rowan Atkinson and Richard Curtis in a room. And whenever I did see people like that I kept imagining a frame around them, like I was watching through a screen. All the *Inbetweeners* boys bonded over our massively nerdy, encyclopedic knowledge of British comedy so we navigated that evening walking around together whispering 'That's Rhys Shearsmith', 'That's Graham Linehan' like we were birdspotters or something. It's bizarre.

★

I grew up watching comedy on TV but also stand-up specials on video. Lee Evans in the 1990s was just on another level. His *Live in Scotland* show, which came out on VHS in late 1999, is the best stand-up comedy show I've ever seen. But I think Steve Coogan is my hero of heroes. There's just no one greater at what he does. And the impressive thing about Steve Coogan is that he's an amazing actor, not just a comedy actor. Finding the truth and making something truly believable through your performance so that whoever's watching it is completely immersed is some skill, and he has that in spades. Plus, he's the funniest person ever. If I could build a comedic actor, Steve Coogan is what I'd end up with. He's perfection. And he's set the standard. There are a lot of fantastically funny performers out there, but Coogan is on another level in my eyes. He founded Baby Cow Productions in 1999 with his writing partner Henry Normal, and they've been executive producers on some incredible shows, like *The Mighty Boosh, Nighty Night* and *Gavin & Stacey*. I worked on a show called *Zapped* that was produced by Baby Cow. I've got a lot of friends at Baby Cow now and they let me use their offices sometimes if I'm developing or writing something. A couple of times I've been in the writing room there and Steve will come in and have a little nosey around, asking what we're working on. So I run through it quickly and his eyes light up and he says something like, 'Yup – I like that idea, it's good. What you could do is add this bit, or introduce this character, or have this character go here.' You just sit there for a few minutes and he fleshes out three ideas on the spur of the moment that are all brilliant. And he inspires the people around him to think in a similar way, so you end up learning a lot from him. I think he appreciates that he's got things to pass on and teach to the next generation of comedic actors.

He's always in touch with what's happening now and what's coming up. I really admire the subversive, edgier, less comfortable stuff that Baby Cow does. And for Steve, I suppose all that began with *On the Hour*, the genius radio show that ran from 1991–92 and was transferred to telly as *The Day Today* in 1994. Partridge's first appearance was on *On the Hour* and there was such an amazing bunch of writers and performers on that show, like Chris Morris, Armando Iannucci, Patrick Marber, Rebecca Front and David Schneider. They're super-sharp people who can observe something and put it in a way that's accessible and can be understood by idiots like me even if they are complex ideas. But the courage that people like Chris Morris showed back then, I feel like we're just so far away from that now. I think a lot of comedians feel like it just isn't worth the hassle to lose your career over something that's pushing boundaries. For someone that comes from a comedy background and so looks at the social commentary and gets my cues from comedians and takes a step back from the world to look at it more clearly, I don't much enjoy what I see these days. I can't think of anything current that really makes me laugh.

I do find it really odd now whenever I work on something that people take everything seriously, take time to learn their lines, pay attention and stuff like that. It's really bizarre and they're doing it all wrong. That way, you won't have nearly as much of a laugh as we had on *The Inbetweeners*. We did get told to calm down a lot by the producer. Damon and Iain were supposed to be the grown-ups – they were the creators, writers and executive producers, so everyone answered to them – but they were involved in all the jokes and messing about on set and we'd all wind each other up. It became difficult to take anything seriously when someone said, 'Right, we do actually need to get this shot now because the sun's going down and if we have to do this again, it's going to cost thousands of pounds!' Once *The Inbetweeners* became successful, we used that fact as an excuse to have a kind of muck-about vibe on a working set, when everyone else was turning up each day and doing their jobs. We would say 'This is our process to get the energy we need into the roles. And people love it and can tell that we're mates. And it works, so let's not mess about with messing about.' And looking back, that was probably bollocks and we maybe could have done it a lot better if we'd paid attention and actually worked. Or maybe not, I don't know!

In my spare time, when I wasn't working as a kitchen fitter or working acting jobs, I used to go down into the basement of HMV on Oxford Street where they had their vinyl singles for about £1.99. I think the labels would release singles like this and if they sold well, they'd re-release them on CD. But you could go in there with a tenner and come out with five or six new vinyl singles and their B-sides, so you'd end up with around fifteen tracks. It felt a bit like the music equivalent of a pick 'n' mix store (remember them?) and you'd come out with physical copies too! Although no one ever used the expression 'physical copies' back then. It's a hindsight phrase we've come up with just to distinguish from owning something completely invisible.

I had an obsession with all sorts of music from a very young age. I used to love film scores, like John Barry's *Dances with Wolves* soundtrack and Hans Zimmer's *Gladiator* score. And I see that same passion in my kids now, who love all sorts of different music and have done since they were really young. I play them songs all the time that I think are great and they will tell me what they really think about them, which is brilliant because it means they do have an opinion about music. And that really matters to me, because that's how I felt when I was their age, but I didn't find many people around who thought that way. Although the kids do make me feel like an old-timer. Recently, while going through some of our old stuff, I found my old little blue iPod Mini, which I'd bought back around 2003 and it had 'Live Forever' engraved on it. I told Harrison later that I had found my 'old iPod'. And he went, 'Dad, it's called an iPad' like I was an absolute moron.

★

Christmas with the Buckleys

Putting the Tree Up

Clair: Christmas begins with me asking James to go to the garage to get the decorations and the tree, him having a tantrum and returning about an hour later.

James: I can't believe we're doing this again. I've just put it down! First things first folks: get your gloves on when you're handling the tree.

Clair: That's right – you've got to make sure your little actor hands don't get hurt.

James: And whatever you do, make sure you don't crumple the rug when you stick the Christmas tree base down.

Clair: I can't stand a crumpled-up rug.

James: We've actually had to turn programmes off the telly if there's a rug in a scene that's a bit crumpled. So, when you're assembling your tree, remember that the base is the biggest bit and the tip is the littlest bit.

Clair: But the tip should go in first, surely.

James: I wouldn't know mate!

Clair: Then you get to work fluffing the branches out. Although each year, I forget to do this before we've actually assembled the tree.

James: You've got to watch your own vlog, Clair.

Clair: I do – it's the best thing on YouTube! So we had a fake tree for a few years that we bought from B&Q, but we all loved the idea of a day out to pick a real tree, tying it to the roof of the car and bringing it home to decorate. So we did! We planned the whole day out. But we got it too early in December and it started to die before Christmas. I kept on having to hoover up the needles, and then one morning when I woke up, my fingers felt really tight as if they had elastic bands tied on them. They looked a little bit swollen and red too, but I couldn't really tell. Then I got these big blotches on my thighs that went all the way up and over my bum. So I woke James up to ask what he thought.

James: Your eyes were going in different directions and you looked like a praying mantis. Like something from *Men in Black*.

Clair: I called Dr Danny and had to show him my red arse.

James: He's a real doctor by the way, not just some bloke who's come over to have a look at Clair's arse. He's also had a look at my balls, but that's a different story. OK, I'll tell you. I thought I twisted a bollock jumping out of bed too quickly when I woke up late.

Clair: So it turns out I'm allergic to Christmas trees when they start to lose their needles. So since then, we've splashed out on a fancy pre-lit fake one that should last at least ten years!

Yes Days

Clair: One of my most important traditions at Christmas is the Yes Days. On these days, stuff that usually you'd say no to, you say yes to. 'Can I open this?' 'Yes Harrison.' 'Can I eat this?' 'Yes Jude.' As a parent, you do get the instinct to say no because they're opening presents left, right and centre and you want them to actually play with the things they've opened rather than wanting to keep opening more. But at Christmas, I just override that urge and say 'yes'. Not every day's going to be like this so you might as well have some fun. And James and I are the same as well. If it's 12.30 on Boxing Day and I find James cracking open a beer and slicing off a massive chunk of ham from the fridge, any other day of the year I'd be asking what the hell he's doing, but it's a Yes Day, so it's all good. And I'm getting the cheese out of the fridge every half an hour, so if we're allowed to do it, then the kids should be as well. Plus, you don't feel guilty around Christmas, because you just know that other people are up to the same if not worse than you! You're not the only one pouring a second Buck's Fizz and hoovering up the crackers and pâté at 11.30 in the morning. Embrace it!

Christmas Movies

Clair: We do have a few film traditions around Christmas. *Die Hard*'s always the first one we watch in the run-up to Christmas because it's not really a Christmas film. We usually watch that on the day that the Christmas decorations go up.

James: *National Lampoon's Christmas Vacation* is one of my favourites.

Clair: Jim Carrey's *Grinch* and *The Santa Clause* movies get slotted in too. And I'll watch *The Family Stone* when I'm wrapping up presents. The kids like watching a bunch of really cosy Disney films like *Mickey's Christmas Carol*. Harrison was telling me last Christmas that Disney+ had just released a new Goofy mini series and that because 'at home' was in the title that they'd nicked our vlog name! *Home Alone* (what a classic that is) gets saved for the twenty-third of December and then *Home Alone 2* is our Christmas Eve movie. *Home Alone* is just the best one for a family. Me and James love it and so do the kids. It's one of those films where you're giggling even though you know what's gonna happen. It's the best.

James: Trying to pick between *Home Alone* and *Home Alone 2*, what a nightmare. Your gut says the first one, but then all the amazing things about the second one keep growing in your mind. Running around New York, the Plaza Hotel, Tim Curry's performance and, to be fair, all the catchphrases we remember are from *Home Alone 2*, like 'Wow! What a hole!' And sometimes you notice a line that had somehow bypassed you despite seeing the film about a hundred times. Like when Harry flies through the air on that see-saw thing outside Duncan's Toy Chest and smashes through the roof of a car. You expect his compadre, Marv, to offer some words of comfort, but he comes up with: 'I twisted my ankle on that board there.' Cracks us up.

Clair: Actually, you know what – the two films are neck and neck for me.

James: It's like *The Godfather* and *The Godfather Part II*. I can't pick between them. You could have a gun to my head and I couldn't pick between them. You know Trump only let them film *Home Alone 2* in the Plaza if he could be in the movie. And Richard Branson's always turning up in films, particularly in airport queues in the background. When we were shooting the second *Inbetweeners* movie and had to all fly out to Australia, the producers did a deal with Virgin so me, Joe, Simon and Blake shot a video for the staff of Virgin at their headquarters. We got to use their escape chute at the hangar with a cross-section of one of their planes.

A Little Something for Santa

James: Oh and for Santa, we put together a tray with a carrot for Rudolph, two cookies and a jug of milk, although I've heard Santa would prefer a can of XXXX Gold or a Stella. Clair actually got me a Stella Artois candle for Christmas in 2020. It wasn't actually a Stella-scented candle, it was an empty Stella bottle that had been chopped in half and then someone stuck in a lemon-scented candle. I would like to have a candle that smells of Stella though.

Last thing to remember. Next year, I'll finally record the next Christmas No. 1 single entitled: 'It's Christmas Time, Everybody's Feeling Festive'.

My dad fancied himself as a bit of a guitar player and he's got a really great record collection. He bought a lot of original records in Ireland and in south London when he was younger. I used to go through his records when I was maybe eight or nine and listen to bands like Guns N' Roses, AC/DC and Cheap Trick and artists like Lou Reed. His second studio album, *Transformer*, was produced by David Bowie and Mick Ronson, who also played lead guitar and piano. And you know how everyone remembers an album that your dad would play in the car on the cassette deck to and from a holiday? Well, *Transformer* was my dad's one. And to be fair, it's a blinder. But he had a few misses as well. He was really into Chris Rea and *The Road to Hell* would be on a lot when we were on our way to a caravan park somewhere. And I'd be thinking, *Maybe we could listen to the whole album just once and then put something else on?!*

When I was seven or eight, we did a class project at school on the 1960s and that's what got me obsessed with The Beatles. I remember being amazed, thinking these guys are so cool and everything I wanted to be. My first two records that I wanted and my mum bought for me were The Monkees' *The Greatest Hits* and The Beatles' *Past Masters, Volume Two*. And I appreciate that they're probably weird choices for a kid's first records. In hindsight, that was pretty cool, but don't get me wrong, I still had the Spice Girls' first album, Eiffel 65's single 'Blue(Da Ba Dee)' and Mr Oizo's 'Flat Beat' – the one with Flat Eric nodding his head along to the beat. So I didn't get away squeaky clean by any stretch. But I did have some credit in the bank with The Monkees and The Beatles.

There was something about music that really spoke to me and no more so than when I first heard *Definitely Maybe*. Liam and Noel Gallagher made me feel like it didn't matter where I came from. And that hit me at a time when I didn't enjoy school and I didn't like being poor. They made me think that there was a world out there waiting, beyond my terraced house. And there's nothing wrong with a terraced house or working a steady 9 to 5, and a lot of mates grew up doing exactly that type of thing and many of them have done really well, owning their own construction companies, but it just wasn't for me. It's not that I thought I was too good for it or anything like that; it just didn't interest me. I just really wanted to get out and do something special. Television and music all reminded me that there was something else out there and I wanted to be a part of that. And I felt so frustrated, as an eight- or nine-year-old, that I was too young to do anything about it. I kept thinking to myself, *Look at all the fun they're having!*

About a year or two after I left school, I found out that a mate of a mate called Matt (who's now one of my best friends) was playing bass in a band with a couple of his other mates. He was a guy that I'd run into from time to time through friends and he knew I was massively into music. Well it turned out they needed another guitarist, so we started rehearsing in a place called The White Room Studios in Rainham. The band that all of us loved was Oasis so essentially we were a bad Oasis tribute band. We'd always do a cover of 'Cigarettes & Alcohol' in our set list. At the time, I thought what we were doing was great, but in hindsight, I can appreciate that we weren't actually that good.

It was almost like play-acting being in a band. We never really recorded anything or got any serious interest but we played a few gigs at bars and occasionally we'd play in London. We played the Mother Bar once or twice in Old Street. Unfortunately, I decided it wasn't what I wanted to do for a career, but I got to play music with guys that I liked and it was just a little adventure really. The furthest we went was Bristol, which felt like a big deal at the time.

As soon as I started making any sort of money at all from acting jobs, music is what I'd spend it on. I'd go to HMV and look for indie labels and bands that I might like. Sometimes I'd hear them first on the radio or MTV2. MTV2 (called M2 when it first started in 1996 before it was rebranded) used to debut new independent bands every Friday evening that no one had heard of and Vampire Weekend came on in early 2007. It used to be such a hobby of mine listening to these new bands and telling everyone that 'these guys are going to be big, watch this space' or 'I'd put my house on these guys being the next big thing' and then being wrong 99 times out of 100.

There was an indie label called 1965 Records that I absolutely loved. They signed some amazing bands like The Draytones (an indie rock band who headlined at Glastonbury on the Thursday night slot back in 2007). They had a song called 'Keep Loving Me', which reminded me so much of The Beatles and made me realize that there were bands around that I really liked. The Metros were an amazing indie punk band from Peckham and their song 'Last of the Lookers' is amazing. Ripchord were another band 1965 Records signed, an indie rock band from Wolverhampton, and then there was The View, who were probably the most successful of the lot. 1965 Records released most of their artists on vinyl singles, so I'd find them in the basement at HMV and pick them at random or have a flick through the covers and pick one where I liked the cover art. Sometimes I would have heard one of their songs already and I wanted to find out more about them. The single vinyl release thing was probably a kind of old-school marketing thing but that retro vibe worked on me. And I thought I was dead cool.

I got really into bands and guitars, going into London and spending the night at indie clubs and finding other people who were really into the music as well. I'd hear something for the first time, love it and then meander through the crowd to go up and pester the DJ to tell me who that was I just heard. I remember phoning up HMV after I'd heard a song on the radio and trying to describe, hum or sing the song because I wanted to buy it but didn't know the name of it. *Fonejacker* actually did a prank version of this, ringing up a record store's classical music department and then humming/singing nonsense lyrics to the song 'West End Girls' by the Pet Shop Boys.

It was such an exciting time for music then around 2006, just before the Internet seemed to provide everything and buying actual copies of things started becoming a thing of the past. But not to me and Clair!

★

James's Desert Island Discs

I've tried to pick songs where there are actual reasons why I've chosen them instead of saying 'Because it's just such a good song.' So here goes.

'God Only Knows' by The Beach Boys

I just think it's the most beautiful love song, ever, by songwriters Brian Wilson and Tony Asher. And the juxtaposition of the lyrics which at first seem confusing but then they're beautifully explained. The song kicks off with 'I may not always love you' and the first time you hear it you're thinking, *Where are you going with this?!* but then they follow it with 'But long as there are stars above you / You never need to doubt it'. Just an absolutely amazing song. It captures the feeling of falling in love with someone and it does remind me of Clair. I know, just like everyone else knows, that someone has never loved someone else as much as I love Clair. It's a big song for us, but it didn't quite make the cut for our wedding song. On the inside of our wedding rings, we both got words engraved and kept them secret from each other. Inside mine, Clair had 'You Do Something To Me' inscribed, the title of, and lyric from, the Paul Weller song that we had for our first dance at our wedding. And inside Clair's wedding ring is 'God only knows what I'd be without you'.

'Men's Needs' by The Cribs

This song just reminds me of being young. In my late teens and early twenties, I thought The Cribs were the coolest band in the world and I just wanted to be mates and hang out with them. Their albums just kept getting better and better and the third one is absolutely brilliant. I think I'd done a series of *The Inbetweeners* when I heard that album but I still didn't have a proper career in acting ahead of me by any means. I was still convinced I was going to be in a band.

'Growing on Me' by The Darkness

At school I played the guitar and when I first started secondary school there were a couple of the older lot that were always in the music room playing guitar and drums and stuff like that, so I had a year of that and by the time I'd got into Year 8 they'd left and the closest to an instrument that anyone at school seemed interested in was the decks (Technics 1210s and stuff like that).

So I was always a bit old school and a bit odd being really into guitars. I used to spend lunch and breaktimes by myself in the music room playing guitar and a few times I was called a 'grunger' by other kids. Which didn't make much sense really because, while I do love Nirvana, Alice in Chains and Pearl Jam, I was spending much more of my time listening to Britpop and sixties music. When The Darkness started to become well known in the early 2000s and there was this sort of seventies glam rock, spandex and catsuit revival, I couldn't believe my luck. I was thinking, *This is incredible that this is happening right now!* I still love their debut album *Permission to Land* (2003) and I don't care what anyone has to say about that. If you like guitar music then it doesn't really get much better than that when you're there watching it. They weren't a band that my dad would have been listening to as a kid. It felt like it was written for me and that felt amazing.

'Little Wing' by Jimi Hendrix

I realize that a theme of my chosen songs is that I'm a sucker for a great guitar sound and I don't think a guitar has sounded any better than on this song. It's a delicate song with dark lyrics that I've always found evocative. All right, that's enough of me sounding like I'm writing for *NME*. I love this song so much and the guitar is almost perfection. I don't remember the first time I heard Hendrix but he would have been on in my house when I was growing up. But Hendrix is one of those musicians that feels to me like he's always existed, like I had no memory of a life before knowing Hendrix.

'Perfect Day' by Lou Reed

This was the first song I learned how to play on guitar so that's why it's one of my favourite songs. It got destroyed by Children in Need, which was a massive shame, but the original version is amazing.

'Running Up That Hill' by Kate Bush

There are a few musicians that I absolutely love – Lou Reed, Ian Brown's another one of them, within and away from The Stone Roses – purely because they're completely unique. They have an individual sound, no one else can do what they do and that's probably the reason why no one's really tried to copy them. You can often tell it's them from the first half-second of a song. Kate Bush is one of those people. I love her music and she has a bewitching voice. She kind of sits apart, as well, with unusual rhythms and instruments so you can't categorize her into a genre. A lot of her songs have a story that is very dramatic. She's just an incredible artist, in terms of the look, the sound, the music videos.

'Pleasant Valley Sunday' by The Monkees

For some reason in the nineties, The Monkees TV series was on every weekday at 6.30pm. It was the last show on Nickelodeon and I watched it every evening. I was obsessed with everything about Davy Jones and I wanted to be him when I grew up. And to be honest, I still do! I just love The Monkees so much and, in a way, they were marketed for me to love them. I don't know how I caught it or why Nickelodeon chose to rerun this show from the sixties about a manufactured pop band, but it was on and I was hooked. I love the guitar riff on 'Pleasant Valley Sunday'. They were all brilliant musicians and I imagine it got on their nerves throughout their whole lives that they were pretty much created off the back of the success of The Beatles and America wanted to cash in on a version of that.

'Live Forever' by Oasis

Just the best song ever. I have 'Live Forever' tattooed on my arm, which I got when I was about 19. I don't have a good story behind this one, it's just a brilliant song that makes me happy. I love the composition – it's got some great guitar sounds in it and beautiful lyrics. It's just a perfect storm of everything I want out of music.

The first gig I ever went to was Oasis at Finsbury Park in July 2002. I was 14, nearly 15. The venue opened at 12pm and, having not been to a gig before, I remember thinking I'd have to be there at 12pm as that's when Oasis will be on stage. So we got there at exactly midday. But I'm glad we did because the eight or so hours of support acts were unbelievable. The Coral (they were the first on), The Charlatans, Black Rebel Motorcycle Club, Cornershop, Proud Mary and then Oasis. It felt like about a hundred bands were playing that day. The trouble was, seeing that as your first gig kind of sets you up for being massively underwhelmed the next time you go to a gig. That night, Oasis was the best band in the world and it was amazing. They'd just released *Heathen Chemistry* so they played a lot from that album as you'd expect ('The Hindu Times', 'Force of Nature', 'Hung in a Bad Place', 'Stop Crying Your Heart Out', 'Little by Little', 'Born on a Different Cloud'), but they also sprinkled in 'Cigarettes & Alcohol', 'Morning Glory', 'Live Forever', 'She's Electric', 'Acquiesce' and 'D' You Know What I Mean?'. The encore was epic, with 'Don't Look Back in Anger' and 'Some Might Say' before they finished with a cover of 'My Generation'. Amazing. What I didn't realize is that Oasis gigs have a history of people lobbing piss, so I remember coming home reeking of urine.

'Love Is the Law' by The Seahorses

It's all about the guitar, this one. John Squire (who left The Stone Roses and founded The Seahorses) has been a hero of mine since I was nine or ten. It's always been a battle between him and Rory Gallagher for who is my favourite guitarist of all time. I don't think I could pick from the two of them. It's very rare that I find someone to bond over The Seahorses with. Most people don't know who they are and if they do they don't like them, but one person who does share a love of the band is Harrison. He's even more obsessed with John Squire than I am and all that's done is make The Seahorses more special to me. I was talking to Clair and saying that I've never spoken to anyone before about how much we both love

The Seahorses and now I get to do it with my son. What an amazing feeling. And their album *Do It Yourself* is one of my favourites.

'I Am the Resurrection' by The Stone Roses

Another John Squire song (co-written with Ian Brown), it's just such an amazing song and when it breaks down and the bass slows I get actual physical feelings. When I hear that hi-hat, I feel it. It's just a guitarist, a bassist and a drummer, especially during that section, and they're three musicians at the top of their game.

Weirdly, I met Ian Brown in 2012 and he gave me a KFC Bargain Bucket. I was tempted just to leave that story there, but I reckon you'll want an explanation. It was at a Stone Roses gig in Belfast in August 2012. I knew they were playing and asked my management to sort something out for me, but it was a bit of a long shot. And then suddenly a call came through telling me I'd got two tickets. I was with Clair at a jeweller's shop getting her engagement ring made, but she couldn't come – Harrison was only a baby and we literally had to leave in about 20 minutes to jump on a plane. My mate Olly was up for it, though, and before we knew it we were standing at the side of the stage waiting for The Stone Roses to come on. I remember thinking, *I can't believe my fu**ing luck here!* We met them afterwards and it turns out Ian Brown liked *The Inbetweeners*. We had a chat and then he asked me if I was hungry. I said, 'Yeah! I didn't know I was going to be here tonight, all I've done is travel to Northern Ireland.' So he tells me they've got a spare KFC bucket going if I want it. And I did, so I had it. Ridiculous. But I ended up being really ill that night, which might have been the chicken. But if Ian Brown offers you chicken, you eat the chicken!

'Don't Mug Yourself' by The Streets

I love The Streets, I love Mike Skinner. I'm a massive Oasis fan and I find that a lot of people who are five or ten years older than me say that they expertly capture what it was like to be a young man in Britain at that time. When *Definitely Maybe* came out I was seven years old, so I was too young to appreciate that, but The Streets capture that feeling for me. Mike Skinner is an incredible poet and everything that he said I understood and appreciated. The first two Streets albums – *Original Pirate Material* and *A Grand Don't Come for Free* are just brilliant social commentary on what it was like being a young adult in the early 2000s. And I think 'Don't Mug Yourself' was Mike Skinner's best song. It's intelligent and witty and even though it is both of those things, it's spoken in a language that's accessible to the working class. It just felt like my life in a song at that time.

The first Monkees album did a similar thing to me and that's one of the greatest albums ever made but The Streets were different because they started getting big just as I was leaving school. *A Grand Don't Come for Free* came out in 2004 just as I started working on the TV show *Teachers*. I was 16 and living at the Jurys Inn in

Bristol for a few months where they shot the series. It was the first time I'd really left home properly and it felt like I was really starting my life. And although I was only 16, I'd go out most nights to the pub with other cast members and crew, who really took a shine to me. So it felt like the soundtrack to that time of my life was *A Grand Don't Come for Free* – a concept album with a story that runs through it all about being young, going to the pub with your mates and meeting girls. It was all the things I was interested in at the time and I loved it. It felt like my coming-of-age summer – looking after myself, not really having to answer to anyone, doing a job that I loved and having fun.

I have to give an honourable mention to 'There Is a Light That Never Goes Out' by The Smiths because when I first heard it, as a socially awkward teenager, Morrissey could literally have been singing about me. So I got really into The Smiths for a few years after that, and I loved Johnny Marr because I'm a sucker for a guitarist. I don't remember buying the actual single or album (as in the real physical copy) so I think I must have downloaded the single on Napster. Oh God, I feel old now. My kids are going to have no idea what I'm talking about.

I know I've picked 11 (well, 12 including The Smiths track) rather than the 8 you get on actual *Desert Island Discs*, but there's no way I'm squeezing any of them out of the list. But if I had to save one of them it'd be 'Live Forever'. I don't know the reason why. My brain doesn't know which one to choose, but my heart says 'Live Forever'.

When I wasn't listening to, or trying to play music, I was watching Channel 4 late-night shows. All that subversive, funny, rock 'n' roll stuff, like *The 11 O'Clock Show*, *The Adam and Joe Show*, *TFI Friday* (which had Ocean Colour Scene's 'The Riverboat Song' for its opening), *The Word* – I got obsessed with all of those shows. I remember watching *The Word* and thinking, *When I grow up, this is what's waiting for me. I'm going to be involved in all of this culture.* 'Cigarettes & Alcohol' came on *The Word* and even as young as I was (seven), I don't think I sat there and thought, *This is really good music.* I just sat there completely fascinated by the whole thing and it felt naughty and that I shouldn't be listening to or watching this thing. But that's what made it so appealing. Looking back, though, at that point in the nineties we were out of Thatcherism but still with the Conservatives in charge under John Major. And the things that I was watching on TV and listening to seemed to rage against all that, and I was hooked.

I remember thinking that when I was old enough, everything was going to change and be so exciting because people who thought in a similar way to me were going to be in charge of things. One of the people that poked fun of every and any situation was Dom Joly, and I absolutely loved *Trigger Happy TV*. He did an incredible job of turning what Britain was like in on itself and laughing about it. It felt like he, along with people like Sacha Baron Cohen, recaptured that feeling of being able to make fun of ourselves. And I watched it thinking, *That's what I want to do after I've got school out of the way, make something satirical and subversive, making fun of all of our absurdity.* And it wasn't just TV, it was a new generation of artists like Tracey Emin who were doing interesting, thought-provoking and weirdly access-ible things. It felt like the voices of ordinary people were being heard and they not only made you think about the world in a different way, they also made you feel like you could break out and do something similar.

But in TV, Channel 4 led the way. Back in 2005, I was doing bits on TV but I also needed a job. So I ended up working at the Home Office in Westminster for about a year. Each day on the way to and from work, I'd walk past the Channel 4 headquarters on Horseferry Road and think to myself, *That's where I want to be.* And then, about a year later, *The Inbetweeners* happened and I was there.

It took about nine months after we finished filming for the first series to come out on TV. And when it did, about a quarter of a million people tuned in (remember when people did that instead of watching it on catch-up?!). It wasn't like it was commissioned for another series straight away at all, although they didn't cancel it, so there was the chance that a second series might happen. But we weren't really properly expecting that, so we just went about our business, waiting for the next job to come along. But then E4 repeated the first series and that was when people started watching it and talking about it. I think that was because anyone that caught it the first time round told their mates about it and so by the time they'd rerun the series, loads more people ended up watching it. And then the DVD, which had come out after the series had been first shown in May 2008, started doing really well. It was probably one of the last TV shows around to properly sell a bunch of DVDs. Remember that? The era before just watching whatever you like, whenever you like. At that point, the channel gave the green light to do another series. We did a promo all in slow motion and looking cool getting out of the car. Well as cool as the Inbetweeners can be – and that got a lot more people watching it. To be honest, though, the promo was conceived mainly because there was no way you could show a clip from the actual show during the day!

Around about then, when I was 21, I had enough money to move out and rent a flat but I thought to myself, *I need to keep hold of this money!* So it took a while for me to feel comfortable enough financially to feel like I could actually afford to move out – it was about the time I started getting paid properly for *The Inbetweeners*.

Then, I found that loads of other job offers come off the back of a successful series and you start doing voice-over work and some interesting roles came up. The most amazing of these was being asked to audition for a prequel to *Only Fools and Horses* called *Rock & Chips*. The part was a young Del Boy, which I still can't quite believe I'm saying. I was properly nervous but the audition went pretty well and I got asked back for a couple of recalls. After the final audition, I kept chasing my agent for any news because I wanted to get that part so badly. But the message I kept getting back was that John Sullivan (legendary writer of *Only Fools*, *Citizen Smith* and *Just Good Friends* among others) hadn't seen the tapes yet. It got to a point where my agent told me that I'd know by a certain day. And that date happened to be the same day that Simon Bird and I were meeting in Edinburgh to go and chat to young people about getting into TV comedy and our experience in the business so far, how we'd got into it and stuff like that.

That morning, I arrived at King's Cross with minutes to spare until the train left, so I ran across the station and only just made it, without grabbing any snacks, water or a magazine or anything. Because remember, that was before the era of iPads or even being able to watch things on your phone! So I had about six hours ahead of me of doing absolutely nothing but stare out of the window, ring up my agent repeatedly (whenever I had any signal) to ask if she'd heard anything yet and then anxiously glance at my phone. It felt like the longest journey that anyone had ever taken. And then I finally got off the train at Edinburgh Waverley and my phone rang. It was my agent. My heart was pounding, but she sounded chirpy, and that was because John wanted me to be Del Boy. What a feeling!

The notes that I got back from John (I still hadn't met him at that point) was that he loved how much work I'd put into the character and that I'd clearly done my homework on making sure that young Del was right. And I was thinking, *I didn't put any work into it!* I just grew up watching *Only Fools and Horses* basically every day of my life so far. It still feels surreal that I did that job. And then when I remember, I think, *Yeah, that was pretty special.* It was a dream job working with John Sullivan, just an invaluable experience. He was always on set and knew absolutely everything about the characters, the clothes they wore, the music they'd listen to, the art on the walls, everything. And then he'd point tiny things out that weren't right, like a stray bottle in the background of The Nag's Head. He just knew this universe and everything about it so well. He was so passionate and loved what he did. And I thought, *If I still feel as excited as he does about the business after decades in it, then I've done something right.*

One of the reasons that *Only Fools* is so special is because you come across characters that so many people identify with. So people often say things like: 'My uncle's like Del' or 'My grandad's like Uncle Albert'. That's what John Sullivan was so good at, looking at working-class life, making fun of it and making it funny. He was a genius at giving people their share of the limelight, having characters take it in turns to be the butt of the jokes. It's not always the case that Del Boy's on top. Sometimes he makes an arse of himself, or Rodney's a drip, and Grandad doesn't know what's going on. But they did have their wins, their moments where one of them finishes the episode with the punchline that gets them on top and they manage to get one over someone else. And that's what life's like. Sometimes you're on top and sometimes you're on the receiving end, but it's that balance of being able to have a laugh at someone being an idiot and then have a laugh at yourself when you're an idiot that's so important in comedy. Because if one of the characters just dished it out, with no comeback, they're just a bit of a dick, but with *Only Fools* they share the highs and lows. And that's one of the many reasons it worked so well.

David Jason came along to set and I had lunch with him, Nicholas Lyndhurst and John Sullivan. They hadn't seen each other, all together in the same place, for a while and it felt like they instantly reverted to being these young men again, making each other laugh, winding each other up, sharing old stories about having a nightmare shooting this and that. And I just sat there thinking, *This is mental, how have I ended up here?!* I thought there might be a point where David Jason would sit me down and ask me something like, 'How are you going to do Del Boy because he's very important to me and I don't want you to f**k this up,' but he didn't. He was just happy to be there with the old gang again and have a catch-up. And I was sat there watching it. I'm not comparing myself to David Jason and Nicholas Lyndhurst, but I know something about the strong friendships you form on a sitcom that people like. Me and the *Inbetweeners* boys will always have so much to talk about and to laugh about. We'll always have that.

I remember talking to John Sullivan after we'd shot the third episode and sharing some ideas about a scene with Del and his mum on her death bed and maybe you hear what she actually said. Or maybe she whispers something that you can't hear as the audience. Because it was always such a great call back when Del would say, 'Mum said to me on her death bed...' John was really keen to write one more to tie everything together between the prequel and *Only Fools*. Sadly, John died just before the third episode of *Rock & Chips* came out, which was a big shock. Before I met him for the first time, I thought he'd be an 85-year-old guy that had been in television for decades and they'd kind of wheel him in, but he was only in his early sixties when I met him and seemed fit as a fiddle. He was so young, only in his thirties, when he was doing *Citizen Smith* and started *Only Fools*. We never got to make that final piece of the story. There was talk for a while of other writers getting involved but you can't finish it without John Sullivan.

3

 **Clair**: After I finished school, I went to college in Glasgow to study art for two years, but I dropped out before my third year, and soon after I did, my papa died. I was devastated. We were so close, and I felt myself standing at a crossroads. I realized that I had to get out of my little town for a while so I moved to London on a whim and decided I'd give it a go in a big city. I got a couple of jobs, did a bit of acting, tried to break ground in the entertainment industry, rented rooms and all that sort of stuff and realized I didn't really like it. It was tough, especially alone and far away from family and friends. I decided to go back home, enrolled in college again, this time to do drama (which is what I wanted to do originally but my art teacher at school convinced me to do art instead). Then, before college started, in September 2010, something funny happened.

The third series of *The Inbetweeners* was about to come out and an advert for it came on when I was at my mum and dad's house. I'd heard of *The Inbetweeners* but I'd never actually watched it. But after that advert came on, I just saw it everywhere – ads on TV and whenever I went on Twitter, which was still relatively new then, I saw that

The Inbetweeners was trending and I started thinking, *I don't know what this is but I'm going to have to watch it!* Anyway, the night came when it was coming on but my little sister Rebecca was watching something else on the telly (and she was way too young to be watching it anyway from what I'd heard about it already) so I forgot about it. But that night, I had a dream about Jay from *The Inbetweeners*, probably just because the show was in my head and I'd seen so many trailers that day. In the dream, we were dating and I remember waking up and thinking, *OK, that's a new one!* It's usually Gerard Butler.

Later that day, I was on Twitter and someone I knew was following James and had retweeted something that he'd said. So I started thinking, *It's this guy again, what's going on?* I went on to James's Twitter and started following him and he followed me back straight away and I thought, *That's a bit weird.* I don't know how it happened but we started talking on Twitter and that became exchanging phone numbers and we started texting literally all day. And then I said to him, 'You're gonna have to phone me because for all I know, I could be talking to some weird old guy.' So he phoned me and, you know, James has got a really distinctive voice and I thought, *Shit – it is him!* Because by this time I'd watched some *Inbetweeners* episodes. Actually that's a lie – I'd watched interviews with some of the cast on YouTube. I think it had been on when I was with an ex-boyfriend, because he was a big fan of the show, but I wasn't really watching it. I think I was messing about on my phone. I do ask myself if I would have had the same dream about James if I'd watched *The Inbetweeners* and seen what a little pervert Jay was. I don't know – maybe not!

The funny thing was that when James and I were talking, I didn't actually know what his second name was, but I found out that one of the actors had the surname Harrison. Harrison was always the name I wanted for my kid and I went, *Oh God, I hope it's not him because Harrison Harrison doesn't work!* I was clearly thinking way ahead! James and I started to text each other constantly, call each other in the evening and talk for hours each night. A couple of weeks later he was doing a bit of DJ'ing in Liverpool and we figured that Liverpool was about halfway between Essex, where James lived, and where I was, near Glasgow. So he suggested we meet up in Liverpool in the daytime and have some dinner and whatever. Part of me was thinking this was an insane thing to do, questioning whether or not it was really him and worrying what the hell I was going to do in Liverpool in case it wasn't him or he didn't turn up. But in the end, I thought, *F**k it*. I bought a return ticket in case he was a no-show or it was some weirdo.

Well, I didn't use the return ticket! We did a bit of sight-seeing and went for some lunch. He'd driven up to Liverpool from Essex so he had the car and asked me if I wanted to come with him back to Essex. I thought, *I've got college in the morning but yeah, why not!* My mum always makes the joke that I'm still on my first date because I never actually came home. James was just about to start the Christmas special (second episode) of *Rock & Chips* where he played a young Del Boy. I think he had maybe two weeks before he started that, so we had a whole two weeks together. I wasn't really doing anything and neither was he so we just waited to see where things were going to go. I figured all I stood to lose was my education and my future! I remember my mum calling me back after I told her that I was heading south – she wasn't massively happy.

My mum and dad were always quite strict-ish. With a brother four years older than me and a sister ten years younger, I was the one who got into trouble, a kind of wild child, so I guess they always sort of expected something a bit nuts from me. I was in Essex for about ten days and then James and I booked flights and went up to Scotland. James met my family. My dad, Davie, is a man of very few words, like probably too few (although James does say if he's got something to say, it's probably worth listening to). You don't know if he likes you so he's kind of a typical Scottish dad in that way. And to be fair, I'm a bit like that, which is why I sometimes get called ' Wee Davie' by family and friends, and James.

So my mum meets James and loves him instantly because he is James: sweet and cute and funny. (Now, James gets on so well with my mum, that sometimes if he and I have an argument, he'll call her! Then she'll call me up later on that day and tell me to 'Stop being so hard on that wee boy!') And then my dad came home. I should say he's a massive *Only Fools and Horses* fan and had already watched and loved the first episode of *Rock & Chips*. So it all seemed to go fine, partly because James had played a young Del Boy, and Davie loves Del Boy. Later on my mum told me that once we left my dad said, 'That's the kind of boy I thought she'd bring home.' So he was happy.

When we were talking on the phone before we met up, we spent a lot of time chatting about music and The Beatles especially. We'd already named our first child. We were so comfortable talking to each other but hadn't met yet. I was getting ready the night before meeting him in Liverpool and he phoned me when I was in bed and asked me if I was a bit nervous. And I said, 'Yeah, I am a bit nervous, but obviously I'm excited.' He said, 'Well, you should be nervous – you're going to meet your future husband to-morrow! That's a big deal!' I said, 'Oh for God's sake!' and rolled my eyes (better get used to that eh?). It sounds so corny but we both just kind of knew how this would go. James always says, 'Thank God she had a dream about me because it could have been anybody and she would have married them!'

While this whirlwind was happening, James was getting recognized everywhere we went and it took a while to get used to it. But I can't think of any time where we've been out and it's been a problem. *Inbetweeners* fans are always happy to see an Inbetweener. People grew up with these characters and they love them, and I think a lot of the reason for the success was that they managed to touch on every young British man in those four characters. So many people tell me that one of the characters was so much like their mate.

Although sometimes, people need someone else to tell them which one of the Inbetweeners they are because they don't want to admit which one they are! Something people say a lot that does make me laugh so much, because it's true, is that in every group, especially boys, if you thought you didn't have a Jay in the group, you were the Jay!

But while you might like one of the characters more than the others, there's nothing really that makes you hate any of them. But there is something about Jay, probably because he's so outrageous, which means that people may expect more of James when they see him in public. James always handles it really well, though, especially when it's just someone who is excited to see him. People say lines from *The Inbetweeners* every day that we're out and they have been doing that since the first day I was with James. 'Bus wanker' is probably the most common one. For years I've tried to get James to yell it out of the window when we're driving past a bus stop, but no joy. But I'll keep trying – it would be so funny.

I'll never forget when James and I just started going out and we went to a shopping centre and there were four or five people, like in their seventies, and they were all sitting at a little Costa. Two of them came up to James to tell him how much they loved the show and they were all waving at me. I thought to myself, *Is there anybody who doesn't watch* The Inbetweeners*?!* There was an old guy who showed us round this house when we were looking to buy a place and it wasn't the right one for us but everything was immaculate. He was telling us that his son had helped him tidy up the night before. We noticed that literally only one thing was out of place in the whole house and it was an *Inbetweeners*

DVD on the coffee table in the lounge. But he hadn't said a word about it. James and I kept looking at each other and the three of us kept chatting until it got so awkward that someone had to say something. And only when we pointed it out did the guy say, 'Oh bloody hell, so it is – me and my son were just watching that last night!'

One year, we booked a spur-of-the-moment holiday to Barbados for Christmas week. I was very new to this weird lifestyle where I had to start thinking about the paparazzi. I was pretty oblivious to it at the airport in Barbados when this English guy came up to me and said, 'I think I've missed my resort bus. What resort are you going to?' James had gone to get a trolley for the suitcases so I was on my own. I told him where we were staying and instead of saying something like 'Oh that's not my one' or 'That's my one' like you'd expect, he just said 'Great' and walked away. I told James about what just happened and he said 'I bet that was paparazzi.' My first instinct was, 'Who do you think you are?! They're not after us – give me a break!' But a few days later, we were on the beach and I suddenly saw the guy. James watched him for a while, before he got on a little boat and went way out until you could barely see him. Lo and behold, the next day I got a phone call from my mum saying we were in the *Sun*, the *Scottish Sun*, the *Daily Record* and the *Daily Mail*. And it happened for the whole holiday, not that we ever saw the photographers – I'd just get a message from my mum and we'd look it up online.

This all came at a point where the third series of *The Inbetweeners* had just come out and they were in talks about the movie so the press were interested. In Barbados, one pap did take a picture of James doing this weird kind of movement holding both hands out in the water, but what they didn't know is that he was actually doing the Peter Andre 'Mysterious Girl' thing from the video, which was really funny. If only they'd known that!

I remember the first bad comment I read online about myself was under a picture of me that a paparazzo had taken when we were on that holiday, walking back from a shop. I had no make-up on, my hair was up and I was holding a bottle of Lucozade. The headline of the article was something like: 'Jay from The Inbetweeners with model girlfriend...' and someone had written: 'Model? What does she model – shoes?!' Yeah it was mean but also quite funny to be fair! James told me not to read online comments from then on and I was like 'Right – got it!'

After that holiday I started needing to be aware of my surroundings. The press attention happened when we were back home as well, so I had to remember that even going about my normal business I might end up in a paper. I've got quite thick skin, though, so I never got that stressed about it.

It's calmed down a lot since then but when we were first going out, the show was huge and it was a real culture shock for me. I had to get used to not just nipping out when I was with James, it was always a bit of a debacle but in a good way. Once the film came out, it got even worse.

Barbados with Bob and Babe

Aside from being on paparazzi watch, our Barbados holiday was different for quite a lot of other reasons! I'm not sure what was going on, but we ended up at a resort that was completely full of eccentrics. There was the largest man I'd ever seen in my life, his name was Bob, and we knew that because he had a T-shirt on with the words 'I am Bob' written on it. His wife was there, who wore a T-shirt with 'Bob's Babe' on it in the same font, and they'd clearly got them made specially for the holiday.

Usually, you might choose to avoid folks like that, despite the fact you see them all the time because you've all arrived at (and will be leaving) the resort at the same time. But we kept getting roped into activities like a game of water volleyball with Bob, his babe and some other people that made me and James think we were in some kind of weird sitcom. James seemed to be enjoying himself though and ended up taking the game really seriously, which was hilarious. He kept doing this thing where he'd be wandering around the pool, looking down, really concentrating and saying 'Right' to himself. After hearing him say it about 20 times, I went up to him and said, 'Right…what?! Who are you talking to?!' And then he started laughing because he hadn't even realized that he'd been doing it. He still does it though!

The pool seemed to attract some weird behaviour. I remember we were just chilling out, reading on the sun loungers and some of the guys that worked in the bar came up and gave us a completely random certificate for 'Best Couple in the Resort'. James and I looked at each other trying to process how we'd won a competition for something that (a) we didn't know we were in and (b) didn't actually sound like anything anyone would ever organize a competition for. So we looked at each other, confused, and said, 'Er, cheers!?'

We were walking close to the pool together one night and I tried to push James in but it didn't work, his sticky feet kept him glued to the floor! And then this big grey monkey appeared out of nowhere around the other side of the pool. I said to James, 'Monkey – there's a monkey running around!' And he was like, 'Yeah, yeah, all right, Clair.' So when he looked round and did actually see a huge monkey, he nearly crapped himself.

One day we woke up and there was this utterly crazy rainstorm and the whole hotel room flooded. We had to walk across the street to get some food, because they'd closed the hotel restaurants, and the water was literally up to James's waist so he had to give me a piggyback. We came back to the room and about half an hour later we got little leaflets through the doors saying: 'Do not cross the road' because someone had just fallen down a manhole and got seriously injured. Luckily we went before that, because I needed my Lucozade and crisps!!

Also, I may have broken a jet-ski while we were there. It was the first time I'd been on one and I got way too cocky. James stopped on his jet-ski and was kind of bobbing around. So I did that thing where I was revving up before going straight towards him full throttle. I planned to stop or swerve at the last minute, but I hadn't worked out which one I was going to do so just ended up crashing into him. And the front bumper of the jet-ski fell off. James has never got over that and every once in a while says, 'What were you thinking on that jet-ski?! Why did you…' and I still don't know. There was a glitch in the matrix somewhere.

James: If you'd have told me when we started filming series one of *The Inbetweeners* that three and a half years later we'd be in Magaluf, Majorca, shooting the movie, I'd have said you were mental. But against the odds, it was successful. Back when we did that, the idea of making a film spin-off of a TV show was crazy, but I think thanks to *The Inbetweeners*, the idea doesn't seem as silly any more. To be honest, I'm still not sure why the film worked! They were talking about making the film while we were shooting series three of the show but it wasn't confirmed until the last minute, just after we'd finished the last episode of the TV series. We went to Malia, Crete, to shoot a little taster for the film, walking in slow motion (again, but it's always funny) along the strip. We shot that bit (which did make it into the film) while it was summer season out there and it was full of people who'd watched *The Inbetweeners*. We had to hire security because people were so excited to see us and that was the moment I think me and the other boys realized that *The Inbetweeners* had become a big deal to quite a few people.

Buckley's BBQ Marinade

I like marinating steaks (I tend to go for sirloin) for as long as possible before firing up the BBQ. Usually it's two days but always at least 24 hours. And whenever I make this marinade, which I've nicked from somewhere and adapted, people are proper impressed (even Clair). It's well easy and it's well tasty!

80ml (16 teaspoons) olive oil

40ml (8 teaspoons) balsamic vinegar

40ml (8 teaspoons) Worcestershire sauce

40ml (8 teaspoons) soy sauce

As much garlic powder as you fancy (we use a lot in the Buckley house)

Mix everything together in a plastic container big enough to hold your steaks.

Whack your steaks in the marinade and slosh them around, stick a lid on and put it in the fridge until tomorrow. Whenever you remember to, take the box out of the fridge and give it a shake.

I like this to be timed to perfection, so I start heating up the coals at the same time as Clair puts some potato wedges in the oven. Clair handles the wedges, I handle the meat. Stick to your specialities. I'm a good meat handler. ;-)

So, the first thing I do is to chuck a couple of tumbleweeds, which are like natural fire starters, into the BBQ. This is the best way to get your coals to catch without having to use any firelighters. Leave the tumbleweeds there for about 20 minutes or so until they're red hot, then dunk your coals in, put your grill on the top and you're laughing.

I stick the steaks on for 5 minutes on each side over a direct heat. All those flavours from the marinade will be in the meat and it'll taste absolutely amazing.

As for the second film, we really were just pissing about constantly for the whole shoot. We knew it was going to be the last time we did anything properly Inbetweeners-wise, so we just really enjoyed it. We had such a great time, and we got to be in Australia, which was just amazing.

What I didn't know before we arrived there is how massive *The Inbetweeners* was in Oz. It was probably the closest I'll get to experiencing Beatlemania when we got off the plane! We were getting stopped all the time by people who wanted to talk to us and get near us way more than back home. Everyone seemed so pleased to have us there, they were so welcoming and just up for a laugh. So all of that made for such a fun last hurrah. It was my favourite experience of the whole Inbetweeners journey and made us feel a sense of 'Let's do it'. It's a huge country and I had no idea how something I was part of had such a big effect on people so far away. In the end, Australia was like a fifth character in the film. And I got to work with, and I still believe this, the three funniest male actors my age. It was an absolute dream. And people still like it and I think it still holds up, which is a bonus.

I didn't spend that much time thinking about what a quick transition it was, though, between occasionally getting recognized and then everyone knowing your face. But if I thought about stuff like that too much (which I have done), I would go insane, so I try not to. But I'm happy to have a chat with anyone if they want to talk about *The Inbetweeners* or anything else. I'm always thankful to those people who went out and watched it and bought tickets to see the films. The only time things are different, when I like to keep my head down and get to wherever I'm going, is when we're with the kids.

The Kids

Clair: I never really imagined having girls when I started thinking about becoming a mum, although I had picked out 'Eleanor' in case we did have one. I didn't grow up playing with dolls and talking about wanting to be a mummy, but when I got to 12 or 13, I did always say if I did have kids, I'd want two boys. That's just what I pictured. I knew I'd call my son Harrison. After George, of course. When James and I were in the labour ward the first time, we'd brought along an iPod with a Beatles playlist (only Beatles!) and an external speaker because I wanted that to be the first thing the baby heard. Harrison's first song was 'Sgt. Pepper's Lonely Hearts Club Band'.

Twenty-one months later, when the second trip to the labour ward came around, we hadn't actually decided on a name yet. But when he came out, it was this really surreal moment, because as they wrapped him up and gave him to us, in that classic *Lion King* moment way, we heard 'Hey Jude' from the speaker. So James was like, 'Oh my God, it's Jude!' At first I wasn't that keen though, so it took a couple of days, but in that time James was already calling him 'Baby Jude' all the time. And so was Harrison! So I got on board.

Buckley Bakes: Jude's Triple Trouble

Our Jude came up with this recipe on a rainy Sunday morning while watching *Bake Off*. (Has James mentioned he won Star Baker yet?)

This undisputed classic in the Buckley household is made from three plain digestive biscuits that are held together with Biscoff spread on one side and chocolate spread on the other. Think of the chocolate and biscoff spreads as the mortar holding them all together.

Instructions for eating: treat it like a Big Mac. Hold it vertically and get stuck in!

Jude made me laugh recently after I picked him up from school. 'Hey Jude' came on in the car and he was all happy talking about his song. And he loves to hear the story about how he ended up being called Jude so pretends he hasn't heard it before, so I tell it to him again, about how the song started playing just as he was born. Jude paused and said, 'So, Paul named me.' And I was like, 'Well, yeah, I mean, I had to make the decision, but you could say that.' And I know what this is really about – Jude wants to go into school and say

'Paul McCartney named me.' He's reaching but you can't blame him for wanting to conjure up a link between him and The Beatles. So then he asks me how old Paul McCartney was when he was born, so I looked it up and did the maths and it turns out he was 64. And both Harrison and Jude gasped and started singing 'When I'm Sixty-Four'. Jude's taken it as this cosmic, everything's falling into place kind of moment. And meanwhile, Harrison's convinced he's George Harrison reincarnated. Both of them take every little thing and run with it. I have definitely accomplished my mission of making sure I'm raising Beatles fans.

We went up to Scotland to have both of the boys. Everything's a bit smaller and quieter and you usually have your own room. And your own midwife the whole way through, which is so lucky.

With Harrison, back in October 2011, I remember waking up one morning and not feeling quite right. Nothing crazy. No big cramping or anything like that but something weird was happening. But I couldn't explain it. So I went to hospital and they examined me. Weirdly, James was talking to James Corden while this was happening because he (James Corden) was doing a play called *One Man, Two Guvnors* at the National Theatre and my James was supposed to take over from him in spring 2012, so they'd been talking quite a bit. That night we were supposed to be seeing the show because it had gone on tour and was in Edinburgh for five nights. So we were in the hospital that morning, and after the examination the doctor tells me there's baby poo coming out. That's right, my baby had shit inside me. I heard James laughing from behind the curtain. But then the doctor said, 'But that means we're going to have to get him out of there.' And then James sort of went quiet. And I said, 'OK. When?' And the doctor said 'Now!' Then I heard James (still behind the curtain) saying, 'What?! We're supposed to go and see a play tonight!' My first thought was, *Well, you can go if you like, but I'm f**king busy!* Then the doctor, who probably read my expression correctly, pulled back the curtain and said, 'No play. Baby!' So, James was like, 'Oh right, OK, I better go and make a call.' James had to go back to my parents' place, grab all my stuff and get back to the hospital before it all kicked off. But James was panicking and when he got there and started frantically rummaging around, my mum asked him what was going on. And he said, 'The baby's shit. It's shat. It's shat inside her. We've gotta get it out!' So my mum was like, 'OK, relax, it's gonna be OK.'

After that, they had to manually burst the waters and it was about a 16-hour labour. I wanted to be on the bouncy ball, but they needed to monitor the baby for a lot of it, so I had to be lying down, which was a bit stressful and uncomfortable, but fine in the end.

After we had Harrison, we stayed with my parents up in Scotland for about a month, seeing my gran, all my aunts, my sister and my brother all the time, before driving back to England, the three of us. It still felt like a whirlwind of everything happening so fast. I remember putting this tiny little baby on the bed in our flat, looking at each other and having the same thought: *Holy shit, this is us now! We need to keep this wee thing alive!*

By the time Jude came along, who was born only 21 months after Harrison, I felt like I knew what I was doing. I woke up in the middle of the night and was having contractions so woke James up and told him what was going on. I phoned the hospital and they told me not to come in yet until the contractions started getting closer together. By the time it got to the afternoon, I was bloody starving. So we drove to Frankie & Benny's, had some food, went back home and were about to go to bed, but then suddenly, at about 8pm, the baby just went mental and I started feeling like I could push, so we had to go! We drove to the hospital in a panic and Jude came along within an hour. Jude was actually born within the amniotic sac. I didn't know that could even happen at the time, but it's called being born en caul and only happens in like 1 in 100,000 births. Apparently back in medieval times, it was associated with good luck and protected the baby from drowning. I've always thought of Jude as a little angel from that moment, compared with Harrison who shat his way into the world!

Two very different children and two very different stories, each one thinking their story is the better one! They are both the best little boys and I couldn't be prouder of both of them.

★

Quarantine Haircut

James: This is an experience and conversation that I reckon every household in the country has had during lockdown. So the day came when I couldn't cope any longer. My hair was covering my eyes and I asked Clair to cut it. But I was properly scared because the last time she did, I'm not going to lie, it looked a bit weird.

Clair: You know, the first time I did it, it wasn't too bad. The second time was quite good, but the last time it was too long to begin with and it was a bit of a shocker.

James: This time I don't care. I'm on the verge of cutting my own fringe just to get it out of my eyes. I can feel you shaking a little bit.

Clair: That's because I am.

James: It's not making me feel very confident.

Clair: I've had two coffees and nothing to eat so I'm a little bit wired.

[Clair cuts]

James: I can see again!

Clair: You wanna have a look?

James: Uh huh. Yeah, that's good, that! That's really good.

Clair: I think that's the best I'm gonna do and I kinda want to stop while I'm slightly ahead. I'm just going to take a bit more off your fringe. [Keeps chopping]

[Pause]

James: You've f**ked it, haven't you?

Clair: Ooops, I think I f**ked it.

James: [looking in mirror] Yup, you f**ked it. Why d'you do that? Snatching defeat from the jaws of victory?

Clair: I was trying to make it better!

James: The hat'll be back in the next video.

The Proposal

Clair: James took me, my dad and mum backstage to see Paul Weller because we were friends with Steve Cradock (Paul's guitarist and also the guitarist with *Ocean Colour Scene* and *The Specials*). Paul Weller is my dad's hero. He always has been. If there's one person that my dad would ever want to meet, it's Paul Weller. So after meeting his hero, James and my dad went outside for a cigarette and that's when he asked him if he could marry me. And my dad's words were, 'Well I can't f★★king say no now can I?!' Everything just went so well, James fitted in perfectly and everything just felt right.

For the first five years of our relationship, James and I went to gigs all the time, got really close to Steve and his wife Sally and we were at every Paul Weller gig that we could make. That was our thing. It became a case of 'Ocean Colour Scene are playing in Glasgow so let's head up there' kind of thing.

Music is such a big thing in this family and in this house. My dad had a big record player in the kitchen and every house we moved into, there was always a kind of sacred space for the record player. He had a huge collection of music but his favourite band has always been The Jam. My dad even took my mum to a Jam concert at the Apollo in Glasgow for their first date. And when my mum, dad and Paul met and were chatting, my mum told him that and Paul remembered that night because it was the last night they played Glasgow on that tour. I don't think I've ever seen my dad so happy!

The Wedding (Plus a Few Tangents)

Clair: At first, I really wanted us to elope to Vegas and James wanted to have the big traditional wedding, or what he called the Big Fat Buckley Wedding. So I said if we're doing the big traditional wedding, it's gonna be in Scotland. James was fine with that and sort of took the lead when we started planning it for November 2012. We did some Internet research and decided that Dundas Castle looked like the right sort of place, which is a few miles outside Edinburgh. I was worried it might be a bit too big for us, because, well, it's a massive Tudor-Gothic castle. We went to see it and the bit you get married in is the keep of the castle – you go up these winding stairs and it's actually really small. While you could get 75 or so people in there, it felt really cosy. There were candles everywhere and I just thought it looked amazing. I fell in love with it. It was a great mixture of intimate and grand. There were definitely more local venues, Culzean Castle in Ayr was one of them. Other places we looked at were the big hotels that everyone seems to get married in, so we wanted something a bit different. Or to put it in James's words at the time, 'Let's have a proper f**king wedding!'

I had two bridesmaids – my sister Becky, and my best friend Kashka, from primary school. She moved to the area and joined my school two years before we went to secondary school. My primary school was tiny and from nursery until Primary 5 (Year 4 in England), when Kashka came, I was the only girl in my class! Before then, there were 19 boys and me.

Kashka's the sort of person who I won't speak to for quite a bit and then when we do catch up, it's like no time has passed. (To be honest, there's no one that I speak to every day apart from my kids. I'm not one of those mums who's always on the phone to their friends. I don't know where they get the energy if I'm honest! I can barely muster up the energy to have a conversation with James sometimes.) So I messaged her when I was back in Scotland and we went out and had a few cocktails before I popped the question: 'Will you be my bridesmaid?' I said, 'You don't have to though!' She has three sisters and we all grew up together and spent so much time together, it only felt right to have her there.

My family did what we usually do for weddings, which is go to Slater menswear in Ayr and James got involved as well. I told him he didn't need to wear a kilt if he didn't want to, but James was like, 'This is a big traditional Scottish wedding – I'm wearing a kilt!' He was proper into it and loved it, getting a bespoke, tailor-made one. And we've got a tradition up here that once you're married, you're supposed to wear your kilt that you wore to your wedding to every wedding you attend. The trouble is, we keep getting invited to weddings in June and July, and James's kilt was a big, heavy thing because our wedding was in November, so each time the subject comes up I'm like (a) 'You're going to be dying' and (b) 'Are people just going to be like, "What the f**k?!"' (because we're not in Scotland). So he's not done it yet but I know that he wants to. Can someone please invite us to a wedding so he can wear his kilt, bless him?

We had Scottish pipers and Highland dancers. We really

went for the big hoopla. We had chicken and haggis and peppercorn sauce, which was delicious. James loves haggis. It's like black pudding but nicer! With the candles, castle feel and darkness, it looked like a medieval wedding for the ceremony, but the reception was in a huge white marquee (although it was a permanent one with doors connecting to the main part of the castle) and that's when mine and James's personalities came in. We covered the floor in white, hung white curtains and added nice lights so it became a kind of blank canvas for us to work with. And my vision was everything would be white except for green apples to represent The Beatles (after their trademark green apple logo, which they launched in 1968 when they formed Apple Records). Guests' place cards had an embossed green apple on them and then their name in the middle. The menus had the green apple as well and so did the dance floor.

Each table was given the name of a Beatles song. The top table was called 'Do You Want to Know a Secret' (one of the songs from The Beatles' first studio album *Please Please Me*, written by Lennon–McCartney with George on lead vocals). The story behind the top table name goes back to when James was filming *Rock & Chips*. He'd been away for a day and I was in the flat. James sent me a text that just said 'Do you want to know a secret?' I was thinking *What?!* So I replied with something like that. And James answered, 'Listen to that song'. So I played it and it goes: 'Do you want to know a secret?' and 'Say the words you long to hear / I'm in love with you'. And that was how James first told me that he loved me. So I phoned him after I realized and he said, 'I didn't know how to tell you!' It was all very teenage and cute. Makes me sorta sick now.

Our first dance was to Paul Weller's 'You Do Something to Me', which was a decision James and I made early on. It was pretty amazing, then everyone joined us on the dance floor for the next song, which was 'Something'. George Harrison was always going to have a part at our wedding! Later on, a couple of bands played, one of them being The Milk, a brilliant band from Essex that James and I adore, then Ocean Colour Scene played, which was unbelievable. Everyone loved it. As I've mentioned, we've become very good friends with Steve Cradock, Ocean Colour Scene's guitarist. And that first meeting's a funny story...

 **James**: For a while, I did a few DJ sets (well, pushing buttons on a CD player), but it was more like a personal appearance thing. But I didn't want to turn up and just wave so because I loved music I always played songs I liked and put some time and effort into it. I was doing one of these DJ gigs in Manchester in October 2010 and it turned out that Ocean Colour Scene were playing at the O2 Apollo nearby. It just so happened that Clair and I were staying in the same hotel as the band and we both finished our gigs and checked into the hotel at the same time. Mani (Gary Mounfield, bassist for The Stone Roses and Primal Scream, who I think was playing bass for Ocean Colour Scene that night) was there in the lobby and I said to Clair,

'F**king hell – that's Mani!' Then he looked at me, recognized me and said, "Ey, love the show man' and slapped my hand with his great big bass-playing hand. Then, Steve Cradock (Ocean Colour Scene's guitarist, and Paul Weller's band's guitarist for that matter, oh and lead guitar player for The Specials) literally bumps into me in the hotel's revolving door and suddenly he's telling me how much he loves *The Inbetweeners*. It was all a bit surreal. And then it got weirder, because we got chatting for a bit and then Steve mentioned that they were playing the Royal Albert Hall the next night and did Clair and I want to come along? So the next night, we stood on the side of the stage watching Ocean Colour Scene playing the Albert Hall. I've had worse nights. We all got a bit pissed afterwards and Steve's been a friend of ours ever since. We went down to see him, his wife Sally and their kids down at this massive cottage they'd rented when he was working on his second solo album and ended up spending a week there. We've remained really close ever since and Steve and Sally are actually Harrison's godparents.

Clair: That was the first time I'd ever been anywhere near the Royal Albert Hall before. But I did know it from 'A Day In The Life' by The Beatles, because there's the line 'Now they know how many holes it takes to fill the Albert Hall', which is three lines after 'Four thousand holes in Blackburn, Lancashire'. Although

I didn't know that the Royal Albert Hall played an amazingly elaborate April Fool's Day prank in 2015, claiming they had discovered a letter from the Albert Hall's Chief Executive, the fictional Ernest O'Follipar (the surname being an anagram of 'April Fool') to Beatles' manager Brian Epstein from 1967. In the letter, Ernest complained about the 'inaccuracies' in the song 'A Day In The Life', listing three grievances, the first two of which were:

1. That there are four thousand holes in the Royal Albert Hall of Arts and Sciences
2. That the Royal Albert Hall of Arts and Sciences is in Blackburn, Lancashire

He went on to say that the song implied there were four thousand holes in the auditorium, which would 'deter concertgoers who do not want to fall into a hole'. Even more amazingly, he said that after 'lengthy discussion', the Council (of the Royal Albert Hall presumably) had come up with two 'solutions' to protect their business before the album was released on 1 June 1967. The first was a plan to amend the lyrics to keep 'the spirit of the song intact whilst preserving the reputation of the Hall.' And here's what they suggested:

// I read the news today oh boy // another fine Proms season just announced
// And though the concerts can get full // You must attend them all
// Just to go to a concert at the truly magic Albert Hall //

The other 'solution' they came up with was keeping the line about the Albert Hall as it was, but getting one of the other members of The Beatles (they suggested Ringo) to add some backing vocals immediately afterwards. The lyric they suggested was: 'Not that there are any holes in the auditorium, John!'

The Albert Hall even went as far as to forge a cheeky reply from John addressed to 'Prince Albert and friends' thanking them for their letter but telling them that they weren't going to change the lyrics because they liked them the way they were, before finishing with: 'And we won't be saying sorry, because it takes too long to get to Blackburn from our studio at Abbey Road.'

And I bet my Harrison doesn't know about any of that.

Anyway, back to Ocean Colour Scene. I don't think James had been to the Royal Albert Hall before either and we were both so excited. We just clicked with Steve and Sally straight away and we didn't have any kids at the time so we could do exactly what we wanted! After that gig, which was amazing, Steve and Sally took us under their wings and kept inviting us, not only to Ocean Colour Scene's gigs all over the place, but loads of other gigs too that they'd been asked to. We suddenly found ourselves rubbing shoulders with all these rock stars and amazing bands. We went to a few events organized by Pretty Green (the clothing brand that Liam Gallagher founded in the late 2000s, named after the first track from The Jam's *Sound Affects* album). I don't think we said no to any of the things we were invited to (well, the cool ones anyway). Also, at the time James was doing a couple of bits on Channel 4 music shows. So for a while it felt like James and I had been let in to this dream world of gigs and festivals almost every night and meeting all the musicians. But, and I know it sounds like some sort of dramatic cosmic thing that you say, it just kind of made sense given that music had so much to do with James and I coming together at the beginning. Plus, everything had been a bit rock 'n' roll and fast-paced for us anyway, with me moving in with James basically after our first date.

I remember joking with James that 'I don't think we'll be able to stand in the main auditorium again – we're side stage people now, that's how we roll!' It was an incredible time, and it continued when I got pregnant with Harrison. We kept going to gigs, and after he was born we bought him mini ear defenders and took him everywhere! We'd buy him the smallest size band T-shirts you could get at the merch store and he'd be running around backstage with Paul Weller's kids (they are about the same age). We were properly rock 'n' roll for a while, although not at our wedding.

We were so exhausted organizing all the mechanics of the wedding day that by about 9pm we left! I even went up on stage and took the mic to tell people: 'I'm really sorry, it's been so great to see you all and thanks so much for coming, but me and James are off!' It was so early in the evening that it felt a little bit weird, but we were done. Everyone who stayed told us it was one of the best weddings ever, so we're glad they had a great time. We went back to the Boathouse, in the grounds of the venue, which was beautiful. We literally got into bed, watched *The Ricky Gervais Show* on James's laptop and went to sleep. There was no champagne and strawberries, we just conked out.

Just before we left though, the wedding venue had to be evacuated because someone set off a fire alarm! I don't know who was to blame, but I've heard a few names thrown around (well, to be more accurate, one name thrown around repeatedly). Someone else told me they thought one of the kids pressed it. There weren't a lot of kids at the wedding apart from my nephews Ewan and Lewis, Steve and Sally's kids, and Harrison, who had only just turned one, so I'd be impressed if he managed it. It's ended up as a bit of an unsolved mystery because no one ever copped to it. I think someone might have had a cheeky cigarette in the toilet or nudged the fire alarm. There were a lot of guys in bands at the wedding so as the night went on it all got a bit rock 'n' roll, that is until the moment that people were told to evacuate in an orderly fashion.

The morning after our wedding, we got up and had breakfast with our wedding guests who had stayed in the castle for the night. And then James and I got ready to head back to my mum and dad's place. My mum and dad took Harrison in the back of their car and I remember thinking on the journey home, sat next to my husband, *Wedding is over – now I'm just somebody's wife!* It wasn't as much of a comedown as a lot of people tell me they feel after their wedding, though, because me and James were actually quite excited to get back home and chill out with Harrison, order a curry and watch some movies.

Curry Night (i.e. Most Nights)

James: One of the most common sights in the Buckley household is a curry order arriving at the door. We try and have just one curry a week nowadays, but for the last ten years it wouldn't be a weird week if we had three. It got to a point where I'd just ring them up, tell them my name and they'd just bring the usual over.

Clair: That blew my mind the first time he did that.

James: I said, 'Watch this, I don't even need to order' but then I realized I'd need to order for you as well, which kind of f**ked it up. But don't pretend it didn't impress you!

Clair: It did actually.

And this is 'The Usual':

Garlic naan

Onion bhajis

Chips (don't you think about rice-shaming me)

Chicken tikka vindaloo (no potato)

Boiled rice for Clair

Madras sauce for Clair

And here's a handy guide to how you serve and eat it right:

Step 1: Lay out a bed of chips

Step 2: Put the vindaloo on the chips

Step 3: Stuff your big fat face.

After the craziness of the weeks before the wedding when you have to be here, there and everywhere getting everything organized, we just wanted to take it easy and breathe it all in. But having said that, we moved house the next month, so we didn't get to relax for long before the craziness started again and we were surrounded by cardboard boxes.

It had been a packed couple of years: getting together, moving in with each other, having Harrison, then getting married, then buying and moving house, James making an *Inbetweeners* film, us getting pregnant with Jude. It was one thing after another. So, after Jude was born, my mum and dad said, 'OK, can we all relax a little bit now?!' We'd somehow gone from both being young and single to having a house, a mortgage and two kids in just under three years! Mental.

 **James**: We got given a sign that read 'Happily Ever After' as a wedding gift but I remember thinking, *Hmm, that's not really us, is it?!*, so Clair painted it black (with blackboard paint) and wrote something that seemed more appropriate. Quoting The Doors is much more us!

The Kids (Again!)

Clair: From the moment Harrison opens his eyes, the first thing he does is pick up his guitar. I try to get him to eat breakfast and brush his teeth but he can't even hear me because he's already playing The Stone Roses or something. And Jude, well when he's not practising his bass, his thing is drama and he's a little actor. James's agent was really keen for us to sign the boys to her, and to be honest they do keep saying things like 'I want to be in movies' but we just think they are too young. And I know James was already acting at Harrison's age doing *Whistle Down the Wind* in the West End, but things are just so different these days. I think both Harrison and Jude would like to perform but it's a case of finding the right time. I'm not against them doing it, and in a way it would be silly to not let them do it because that's clearly where they're going, but you don't want it to be too early. Having a proper/normal childhood, I think, is very important.

There are so many things about the boys that are so like either me or James and it's so funny when they get to that stage when they're little people and you can talk to them properly and they've got their own opinions. Harrison has never seen a horror film but he's obsessed with the darker side of things, like Chucky. Any drawings or art he does, it's never a rainbow – it's always really weird and dark and possibly slightly questionable. But there's no need to question the parenting, just appreciate the art!

Everyone says the boys have Scottish accents, but Jude sounds quite English to my ear. I've tried to guide him towards more Scottish words, but I've lost him. Harrison's definitely Scottish but he can switch. When he's in Scotland, he talks like me, but when he's at school, he's different. Maybe he's already becoming an actor. But Harrison is a very proud Scotsman and he loves his Scottish history. And I think that's partly because where I'm from – East Ayrshire – has lots of Scottish history attached to it.

Opinion seems to be divided about where exactly William Wallace was born. Some historians think that it was Elderslie, Renfrewshire, which is only about 25 miles north of my home town. But on his official seal, which he used to write letters, he is 'William, son of Alan Wallace'. Alan Wallace lived in Ayrshire, and the Wallace family had estates in Riccarton and Tarbolton – both in Ayshire – so I'm calling him an Ayrshire boy. Whatever the truth about where he grew up though, he certainly got up to a lot in the Irvine Valley. Loudoun Hill is just a few miles away from my parents – I go up there with James and the boys whenever we're up in Scotland – and that's where William Wallace ambushed King Edward I's baggage train. Ten years later, Robert the Bruce, the King of Scots, defeated an English army there despite only having a fifth of the numbers of the English. At the bottom of Loudoun Hill is the five-metre-high *Spirit of Scotland* sculpture, with three inscriptions about Wallace's life. If you've seen the vlog 'Buckleys In Scotland', you'll remember it!

There are loads of monuments around the area commemorating this and that, and Harrison loves that stuff. Until really recently, my parents lived next to a guy called Roger, who's in his eighties. And Roger used to talk to Harrison over the fence about the different stories of Wallace and different battles that had happened around our area. Harrison hung on every word. Roger loved telling his stories to someone who really took an interest.

Both my boys have been watching snippets of The Beatles' documentary *Get Back*. I was worried that it might not be appropriate for the kids because it is four guys chatting in a studio, so I tried to watch it first and check it was OK. But it took so long to watch it all the way through and the kids kept coming in asking if I'd finished, so I just watched it with them. There was nothing that bad in the first hour of it, swearing-wise, and nothing I wouldn't have heard at their age, so I figured it was OK.

We let Harrison watch *Twins* (the 1988 comedy with Arnie and Danny DeVito) recently, which is rated a PG, but there's one moment when Arnie opens a copy of *Playboy* and you see some boobs. I didn't manage to skip it in time and Harrison was like, 'Wooooooooooooooooooahhhhh! I just saw real boobs!' And I was like, 'All right, relax.' Harrison kept looking over at his dad with his eyes wide open. The next night, our neighbour John came over and we had a beer. We were just catching up and Harrison comes in, so John says, 'Hello mate, what you been up to?' and Harrison replies with, 'Saw some boobs last night!' So, then we had to explain to John, who was wetting himself with laughter.

James: Harrison's becoming very accomplished on the guitar already and I don't have the vocabulary to express quite how wonderful that feels. To watch this little thing that me and Clair made, playing the guitar that we bought for him before he was even born, well, life doesn't get any better than that. So that's what I'm chasing now. Both our boys are super-creative and so funny. Jude's a never-ending well of one-liners that just come from nowhere and that you could stick on a T-shirt. But I guess they were going to be creative because Clair and I have encouraged that a lot. The house is never quiet. There's always something on and we're always listening to music, watching films together or playing games.

Thanks to Kats Areallace for suggesting that one for the board!

4

NEW
HORIZONS

Clair: When we first started going out, we were followed by the press quite a bit. I think the fact that Jay from *The Inbetweeners* had got himself a girlfriend was something that people wanted to hear about. James was working a lot then, with *Rock & Chips*, then the first *Inbetweeners* movie, lots of voiceover gigs and adverts, and in between he'd be flying everywhere and doing press events, so I was never really used to him being around for long periods of time. He was always super-busy, which was great. Also, for the past four or five years, he's gone over to LA for a few weeks every year. So we've always had this relationship where James made the money, to put it bluntly (but that's what I do), and I brought up the kids, so if he had to up and leave, I held down the fort. And that's really how his job is. A film can pop up and he can start filming it a few weeks later. I absolutely love being a mum and totally devoting myself to raising the boys is something I know I am so lucky to have been able to do and I cherished every minute (OK, not every minute, but most of them). And that's how it worked and we were both happy with that. Now that the kids are older and I've got the vlog to work on, which really quickly became full-on as James divorced himself from the idea of editing or creating thumbnails or thinking about content or organizing... anything like that pretty early on. But I am really enjoying that now as well.

The reason James has been over to LA for a few weeks each year for the last few years is for pilot season. Before he went for the first time he had to get himself a US agent, which can be quite difficult, so he went to all these meetings. A couple of agencies wanted to sign him and he picked one. Then how it works is that the TV companies (NBC, HBO, etc.) put out all these scripts that have been written to the agencies who represent the actors, and there's a kind of scramble to try and get the scripts to the actors who they think will be right for the roles. James will then get an email saying you've got twelve auditions over the two months and he gets invited to lunches and schmoozy cocktails with casting directors. So there's a lot of hustling involved but he's done well so far. And while he hasn't had his big break over there, he's been in films with some big names and got a part in an NBC show, which unfortunately didn't make it to the second series. Maybe he's been a bit unlucky because we hoped one of the films might have been big enough for something else to come of it straight away.

When James did the *Popstar* movie, which was produced by Judd Apatow (the Emmy-award-winning producer, director, screenwriter and comedian who's done all sorts of stuff, like *The 40-Year-Old Virgin*, *Knocked Up* and *Anchorman*, and is kind of the dream to work with for a comedy actor in America), it seemed like something would come of it but it didn't in the end. Sometimes you just need that little bit of luck, but it's meant we're both quite level-headed and maybe a bit cautious about exciting new parts that James gets. It's really easy to dream and think big, which is a great thing to do, but sometimes that means the disappointment hits harder when it doesn't work out, so I've definitely learned in 'the business' to take everything with a pinch of salt and not to get really excited about something until it's actually happening! (Sort of how I felt about this book to be honest!) James has always said that things will work out the way we want them to in the end. He's got this feeling that we're good people and if we don't screw anybody over and play by the rules and keep being good people, good things will happen. I find it difficult to be on board with that sometimes if I'm honest, because I can be a bit like 'F**k em – just do it!' but James won't have any of it even if we've been a bit unlucky here and there. Nothing will change the way he feels though! And to be fair, I can't fault him so far, we're doing fine.

We got our dog Paisley five years ago and it was mainly because James was away for long stretches and I wanted to feel a bit safer in the house when I didn't have family staying (which I usually do when James is gone). We had her trained properly when she was young, so she's great around the kids but she's just a big puppy really, especially with the boys. However, she does do her job when she thinks something isn't right. There's a funny story from a few years ago that's a great example: our neighbour John was bringing over some parcels for us that had been left with him. It was the middle of summer and the weather was scorching hot so I had opened the living room window. John made his way to our front door and Paisley (not recognizing who he was) started barking and almost jumped out the window at him! John literally threw the boxes up in the air (thank God there was nothing breakable) and ran away! He came back a few moments later, but was talking to Paisley to reassure her it was him, and she had calmed down by then, but John said he thought, *This is it, I'm gonna be rottie food.*

And when she was younger, you couldn't leave anything on the countertop because she'd have it away. She managed to eat almost an entire corner couch over the course of about a month, not to mention a pair of curtains, a couple of stools, countless rugs, at least five pairs of shoes and many wooden table and chair legs. The one that stung the most was when she managed to get a hold of Harrison's Woody (from *Toy Story*) toy. He was absolutely gutted, but thankfully she grew out of the chewing – about a year ago!

Getting used to James being away a lot has meant that I've had to get used to fixing things on my own (actually, who are we kidding, I'd have to do it even if he was here). I probably get my 'fix it' approach from my dad, who'd always be working on something around the house on a weekend. And he'd get my brother Stephen involved, and I didn't want to be left out so I'd be there too, trying to help. I love my painting and decorating, so I do that sort of stuff myself, and getting the place ready for Halloween is always a big deal in our house. Although, having said that, when people who haven't seen us for a while come over (James's mum did once) they often say something like, 'Oh, you've started decorating for Halloween already!' and I'm like, 'No that's just how the house looks!' Because there are always skulls, bats and horror movie trinkets and posters around the place. One of the things that a lot of people comment on is our framed stuffed bat with googly eyes. That purchase started with me in a tattoo shop about to get a tattoo and they had a sort of weird taxidermy vibe in there. And one of the things they had was a huge bat in a frame, so when I got home I typed 'dead bat' into Google, as you do, and bought a stuffed bat. I didn't know that it would have great big googly eyes though, but it does mean that a lot of people comment on it when they come over to our place.

Things go up a notch when Halloween comes round. I treat Halloween like most people treat Christmas, so as soon as it's 1 October I go into overdrive and everything goes up a couple of days after that. I always ask the kids if they want to help or if they'd prefer me to do it so that it's all done for when they come back from school.

My pride and joy is my 7-foot-tall Grim Reaper (known as Death). He talks, his mouth moves and you can set him to be motion-activated so that he starts talking when someone moves near him. This generally scares the crap out of people because they're not expecting it. And to be fair, not many people are expecting a 7-foot-tall Grim Reaper. Harrison was born just a few days before Halloween, and he loves all that stuff, so I actually bought it for his sixth birthday party. He was designed to go outside the door, but he now lives in the living room from the night of every 1 October.

DIY Heroics

Here's how our DIY conversations go in the Buckley household:

Clair: We're going to need to get the drill out.

James: Where do we keep the drill?

Clair: Exactly.

James: I'm a bit wary about DIY. The last time we did some, I nearly got murdered by a picture frame in my own house. It was on a shelf we put up above our sofa in the living room. One day Clair shut the lounge door quite hard, looked up above me and went 'Oh shit!' because she saw that the picture was about to fall off the shelf. But for some reason I didn't think to actually protect myself, I just looked up and then the picture landed on my face. And it reaalllllllly, really hurt.

Clair: You're lucky it landed below your eye and not in it.

James: I could have been blinded!

Clair: You're so dramatic!

I want to give a quick shoutout to Dan O'Shea who made the following comment about James's 'near death experience' after hearing us talk about it on the vlog: 'If only you recorded the picture falling on you, you could have got two hundred and fifty quid because, quite literally, "you've been framed".'

Congratulations Dan, you've won YouTube.

It does take a while to get used to my Grim Reaper though and I still jump whenever I turn the lights on in the morning. He does scare James a lot, but I felt like it wasn't having the same effect as it used to, so I decided to hide it in our little under-stairs bathroom, next to the toilet. I kept forgetting to tell people he was there whenever they went to use it, so you'd keep hearing 'Ahhh, for f**k's sake'. One year, James was working in LA in October and Death was up. Jude was about three or four at that point, and he started hugging Death every day and calling him his dad until his dad came back. So we had to keep him up for much longer than Halloween!

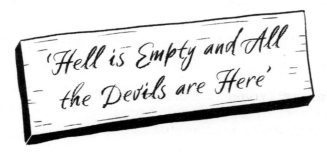

'Hell is Empty and All the Devils are Here'

I used to have certain places for certain things but I stopped doing that because every year I buy more decorations. I don't go completely all out though. If I did, I'd probably have a 20-foot-tall spider completely covering the house in a massive web. And witches suspended from the roof so it looks like they're flying by. The only thing holding me back is my height. I'm very little, so my reach is limited. I did look into getting a company to put lights around the house properly, like they do in the States, but they wanted about six grand to do it!

I think the Halloween thing all started when I was a kid. I remember sneak-watching *Scream* when I was around ten at my gran and papa's house. Sometimes my aunts and uncles would come and stay with them for a bit. My Aunt Joanne and my Uncle Martin were staying in my gran's spare room while they were house hunting and they had loads of videos piled up. For some reason, I kept seeing the ghost face on the cover of *Scream* and I was just drawn to it! I knew it was a scary film and I knew I wasn't allowed to watch it but I wanted to see it so badly and I wasn't sure why! So, I sneaked the video into the video player in the spare bedroom and started watching it, hovering near the door in case I heard someone coming and had to stop it and run out of the room. Watching it that way took me about three days! I absolutely loved it and wasn't scared when I was actually watching it, but going to bed at night I kept seeing the mask everywhere and was too scared to go to the toilet; however I couldn't stop myself from watching it the next day. So that was the first thing I watched where I was scared by it but really enjoyed it. And it's just carried on from there. I'm desperate to find something that makes me feel like I did when I watched *Scream* for the first time. James gets like that though when we watch horror films. And there comes that moment when we'll need to let Paisley out and James will be like 'Er, are you coming with me?'

A few films that got close were *The Strangers* (a 2008 film starring Liv Tyler and Scott Speedman who are at a holiday house that gets invaded by three masked criminals); a remake of a movie called *Funny Games* (a 2007 film starring Naomi Watts and Tim Roth, who are on holiday and get captured by two guys); and *Creep* (a 2014 film, co-written, co-produced and starring Mark Duplass, who plays a videographer travelling to a remote cabin). I love *Creep* – it's so tense and makes you so uneasy. Zombies and ghosts don't scare me – it's people that do. Particularly when everything seems fine and then they get really weird really quickly. Also they're modern and feel that they could happen to you. That's why I'm ready. James thinks I'm mental, but I have all these little panic buttons and escape routes ready! I guess that's what happens to your mind when you only watch horror films!

Then there are just classics that I love, like *Halloween* and *Deliverance*, which is pretty terrifying. I love *The Exorcist* and I can't wait to show Harrison that when he's old enough. It's aged so well – it doesn't look old or shit, it's as amazing as it's ever been. Such an impressive film.

I love nothing more than getting a curry on a Friday night and putting on a proper jumpy, scary film. And when I say jumpy, I mean James jumps.

A Short Story by Clair Buckley

I love horror films. I even got to be in a couple! I've written two screenplays and a few short stories. Most of them were a little too graphic or scary for this happy wee book, so I wrote a fairly tame one for you all.

Her husband waves goodbye from the driveway, leaving her in the mess of her bathroom renovations. Dust is everywhere. Showering is impossible. She is at the end of her tether with it all. But Joe has to work. He doesn't help much anyway. He's a good guy, but a bit of a dick, if she's honest.

Sophia, her eight-year-old daughter, is her little shining light. She keeps her sane. She keeps her going. Balancing work, home, marriage, motherhood and doing it all while trying to eat healthily is a struggle. But Sophia is the reason she can always keep going. Every mother knows that.

As she waves Joe off and closes the door, she sighs a sigh of slight relief. It's Friday. She already has her bottle of wine chilling in the fridge and is looking forward to trying the new Mexican restaurant that has just opened for delivery. It's the little things.

4.45pm. She's in the car on the way home from picking Sophia up from school. 'Let It Go' blasts from the speakers. That Friday feeling has well and truly hit! As she pulls into the driveway, her neighbour and good friend passes by with her dog.

'Hey! Did Joe get away OK this morning?' she asks.

'Hi Lisa, yeah he did. He should be back Tuesday, so I'm just enjoying the peace and quiet.'

'I meant to text you earlier. Does Sophia want to come round tonight? We've just bought Disney+ and Kayliegh is desperate to watch every princess movie with her.'

'That sounds great. I've got nothing planned. When do you want her? I'll drop her round. Will give me a chance to catch up on some cleaning to be honest.'

She isn't going to clean. She is going to open her wine, eat burritos and watch *The Real Housewives*.

'Bring her round in an hour or so? I'll order them a pizza.'

'Sounds great, she'll be chuffed. Thanks Lisa, see you in a bit then.'

She has been friends with Lisa for quite a few years. Maybe six or seven by now. She is a nice person. A good friend. A little pretentious sometimes. But who isn't? Her daughter, Kayliegh, is a good friend to Sophia. Lisa and Mike, her ex-husband, are significantly more well-off than Joe and herself, but anything they bought for Kayliegh she always shared with Sophia. She is definitely a well-mannered, caring little girl, which is why she probably became such good friends with Lisa and Paul, because nice kids are so hard to come by these days.

Mike and Lisa had invited her and Joe on many week-ends away. They had spent a lot of time together as a foursome and always had a great time. The first time they all went away was one of the best weekends she and Joe had ever had. The kids had so much fun and the adults got to really relax and have some downtime. That was in a cabin up in the Scottish Highlands in February. It was a magical weekend.

The second time they joined them in that same cabin was during the summer holidays. That weekend didn't go quite as well. Joe had a face like a slapped arse the whole time and didn't want to join in with any of the activities. The only time he'd muster up a smile and a bit of conversation was in the evenings when the adults were all around the table together having dinner and drinks. Joe is a good man. He provides for his family but he always puts himself first. What he wants to do is what he does. He is a good dad when he can be bothered. But quite often, he can't.

Sometimes when she looks at him, she thinks he regrets settling down with her. He is a bachelor stuck in a husband's life. He seems like the kind of man who always thinks the grass is greener. She used to try to prove to him that it isn't, but after Sophia was born that urge to please him dwindled. Sometimes she wants him to piss off and try the other grass!

6.03pm. She holds Sophia's hand as they walk down Lisa's path. It is an immaculate path. She knocks on her big white wooden door. She can see the chandelier in the hallway twinkling through the glass. Lisa's house isn't her style, but she sure can appreciate how nice it is. As they enter into Lisa's clean, white, dust-free house, she thinks to herself, just like she had many times before, how she'd love to be able to stay on top of her house the way Lisa does. Although Lisa doesn't work. And she has a cleaner. So the game was rigged from the beginning. There are still pictures of Lisa and Mike together in Lisa's hallway, mostly of them with Kayliegh when she was a baby, but she always thinks that is strange. It could be for show? A united front against any nosey neighbours who happen to pop by? It could be that Lisa just doesn't care, but she knows Lisa quite well and Lisa is always up for a gossip. A bitch about someone else and the turmoil they are going through. Who is at fault for it? She loves all that! So it is weird that no one ever really got the whole story about why her and Mike split.

For the past two years since they had been divorced, she could only ever come to one conclusion: Lisa had cheated. It was the one outcome that just made the most sense.

'Hi Sophia!' says little Kayliegh bounding down the stairs towards an excited Sophia. The two little girls share a hug and run back upstairs together.

'Uh...bye then Soph?!' she says, standing at the bottom of the stairs in fake disbelief at how quickly she has been abandoned. She steps forward towards Lisa's kitchen, which by the way is her dream kitchen. Usually at this point Lisa would offer her a glass of wine, but she is stopped in her tracks by Lisa heading back towards the front door.

'Thanks for bringing her by. Kayliegh has been dying to get her back round. Can I give you a call once they've eaten and exhausted themselves?'

'Oh, yeah of course. Just let me know and I'll pop back round and grab her.' She smiles as she awkwardly follows Lisa to the front door. Clearly there is no glass of wine or gossip to be offered this evening. It is a little strange, but she is having Sophia over for a few hours, so she can't really complain. As she steps back out into the chilly evening, Lisa smiles at her and says she'll text her in a few hours. She smiles back and says thank you and goodbye. Still feeling like she was unwanted, but happy to be heading home to crack open her wine and put her feet up, in the short walk back to her house she ponders what she could have done to offend Lisa. There was nothing.

As she turns the key in her front door, she has come to the conclusion that Lisa has probably regretted offering to take Sophia and just wishes she had a quiet Friday night. She puts her phone on the kitchen counter and switches it on to loud mode, expecting a call from Lisa sooner rather than later.

As she opens a bottle of white wine, she slips her shoes off and sinks into her couch, grabbing the remote control on the way down.

A couple of hours pass and she decides against the takeaway – she always feels a bit weird ordering food when she is alone. So she eats her leftover tuna pasta. It is now 8.07pm and there is still no word from Lisa. She decides to send a text: 'Hey just wondering how you're getting on? Sophia behaving? Let me know when you want me to come grab her x'

A few minutes pass before a reply from Lisa comes in: 'Hi yeah she's been great as always. They are fed and have watched their movie, so anytime for pick up is fine :)'

I guess that means now then, she thinks to herself. She puts her shoes on and grabs her keys. She's only had one glass of wine so she'll be fine to drive. She can't shake a feeling of uneasiness that she's had since she left Lisa's house earlier. That she felt quite unwelcome.

Another text from Lisa comes in: 'Hey so they've just asked for some ice cream. I'll give them some pudding and let them play for another hour if that's ok with you?'

She stares at her phone for a few seconds. She is sort of ready to just go grab Sophia and get back home but can't exactly say no to Lisa's message. 'Yeah that's fine, I'll leave in an hour x'

She heads to the kitchen and fills her wine glass. Guess she'll be walking back round to Lisa's.

8.38pm. *BANG!* She jumps upright on the sofa. Then there's another bang from what sounds like the back garden. She stands. Her eyes are wide in her head. She pauses the TV. She replays the sound in her mind. It sounded like something heavy but somehow soft had been thrown against the side of the house or a window. She is frozen, just waiting for the third bang to come. But it doesn't.

She makes her way into the kitchen and turns off the lights. She never understands horror films where they turn the lights on – you can't see what is outside when the inside lights are on! She stands in the dark, staring out.

Inspecting every corner of the garden. Nothing. Rustling bush. Perfect. There's definitely something out there. A fox or a cat hopefully. She looks at her phone. 8.43pm. Almost time to go get Sophia. She checks her doorbell camera. Nothing. She stands alone in the kitchen, gazing at her back garden. She hates this feeling. We've all had it. She's heard two loud bangs but there's no explanation. Like it never happened. And that's the worst. A dead bird on the patio right now would be perfect. A fox running across her grass, anything, just so she can give the noise an explanation and move on. But there is nothing. Just darkness. Very quiet darkness.

8.50pm. Time to go. She grabs her coat and her scarf. She bundles up and takes her keys from the counter, puts them in her pocket and grabs her phone. She opens her front door, a little hesitantly. It's dark, but the street lamps are on. She steps outside and closes the door behind her. As she looks down at her phone, she can see her breath flowing from her mouth. She thinks to herself that she didn't realize it was *this* cold. There's movement. Definitely movement behind her. She should have taken her car. She's perfectly sober. She had two glasses of wine. Why is she walking in the dark? What an idiot. Another glance at her phone. 8.54pm. There is someone behind her. She knows this is a fact now, not just a thought or a fear. She doesn't want to look but she knows someone is there. If she looks then it's real. Her mind is running away with her now. Whatever is behind her is a monster in her mind. She speeds up. Just a little, nothing too obvious. She thinks she may have created more space between her and the monster behind.

This could be a 90-year-old woman on the way to the postbox at the end of the road, she thinks. She is trying to calm her thoughts. She takes a second and turns around, facing the fear. It's definitely not a 90-year-old woman. Whoever it is, is young, fast, tall and wearing a dark hoodie so she can't see their face.

A small turn is coming up, her blood runs cold. This turn takes her into an alleyway. A very short one, but an alley just the same. If she remembers correctly, there are street lamps and it's well lit, but still... *Should I just start running?* she thinks. *What if this monster is harmless? It's not though.* Her thoughts are so loud in her head. She almost wants to tell them to shush. The turn is upon her. She faces the alleyway, trying not to stop, but realizing it is much darker than she thought. Should she skip it? Then she'll have to walk a really long way round.

Stop it. Keep walking. It's fine. She convinces herself, in what feels like ten minutes but is only a few seconds, to continue down into the alleyway. Once she gets to the end of the alley, there is a rather lovely field that always has flowers of some sort growing, no matter the time of year. If she can just get through the alley, she's fine. As she takes her first couple of steps into the dark, she prays the monster behind her will continue on by. It won't even be heading into the alleyway and then she can just calm down. Her thoughts are screaming inside her head: *Don't turn in here, don't turn in here*.

She makes maybe five or six steps down the probably twelve–fifteen-step alley. She hears it behind her. She stops. She turns around. It's behind her. Of course it is. Is it getting faster? She skips into a faster walk herself. The footsteps behind her become heavier, louder. That means they are going faster, right? She makes it to the end of the alleyway. She is about to turn and be greeted by the pretty field. The field where people walk their golden retrievers, the field where the children from the neighbourhood play in the summer, the field where she has taken Sophia many times to pick flowers. She's almost there!

She hears the sound of the hooded monster's trouser legs rubbing together as it clearly sprints towards her. She turns around, instinctively. She knew it. She turns back and runs towards the field. The world around her stops. She can't even see. The voice in her head says: *You knew it. You knew this was going to happen. This morning, when you burned your toast. This afternoon when you clipped your seatbelt in. This evening when you poured the second glass of wine. You knew. You knew all along this was the end of your day. You let this happen.*

Their eyes finally meet as the hooded monster is close enough for her to see it is a man. A man with dark eyes. Familiar eyes. Her head is forced back and her mouth is covered. Is she screaming? She can't tell. She knows she wants to, she knows that she should be. Time is moving like she has never experienced. This is happening so fast, yet so slowly that her thoughts are deafening her. *Your baby Sophia. She's waiting for you*. She thinks about time travel. How, if it were real, she would love to go back in time. A week, a year, a few minutes. But she can't. She's here.

She's at the edge of the beautiful field. The man's grip is tight. She realizes she is struggling to breathe. Her ribs hurt. Her feet feel the ground moving under them, but they aren't walking. She's being dragged into the field, which is much bigger and darker than she ever remembered. Her fear is intense. She has never had so little control. She suddenly feels sick. Like she could vomit. She knows what's going to happen. She always knew.

There's darkness. Not like the darkness of the night but complete darkness. Her head feels really heavy. This seems to last for a long time with no other noise around her. Then there's pain. A pain like she's never felt before. It sort of reminds her of the pain when you banged your head as a child and you couldn't do anything for a few moments, before you'd let out a cry for your mum. A pain where you knew you were really hurt. But somehow, it was worse. Even worse than the time she fell from a high branch on a tree when her and her brother were playing Tarzan.

This pain took her breath away. And her sight. Then her thoughts. For a while anyway. At some point, she can't remember when, but her thoughts come back. And her feelings. She can definitely feel pain again.

A different kind of pain. Her heart hurts. So much that it feels physical but she knows it isn't. The physical pain is gone. Forever.

Her pain is a mother's pain. A daughter's pain. A sister's pain. A friend's pain. For she would never again be any of those things.

Her pain was her own death. And somehow, she knew.

In the run-up to Halloween, Harrison and I always watch *Monster House* (a cartoony comedy-horror about a haunted house), which is really great. And then there's *ParaNorman* (another animated comedy-horror but this one is about a boy who can talk to ghosts) and *Coraline* (a little girl discovers a secret door to a parallel world). And then we'll probably watch *Edward Scissorhands*, *The Addams Family* and *Beetlejuice* about three times each. They're the three biggies in our house. Usually we'll keep *Beetlejuice* for Harrison's birthday, on 26 October, as that's his favourite.

I love Wednesday from the Addams family and have done since I watched the first film when I was a kid. I thought she was so cool – I loved her dress and her hair. There's a bit in the film where she goes to sleep with her arms crossed on her chest and I used to practise that. I was a tomboy growing up and always attracted to the weirder side of things. So I'd watch *The Addams Family* and wish my family was like that. I've never been a goth but I did love wearing black, and still do. When I got to about 11 or 12 and was really into my music, The Jam and The Who especially, and into the mod scene, I was still the weird girl at secondary school but just a slightly new type of weird – not in the dark way, more like 'She's the girl who listens to music from like a hundred years ago and wears a parka' way.

I remember when I was 16 or 17 my friend's dad booked a limo to take us to a big Halloween party. There were a few girls going and I was the last one to be picked up because I lived the furthest away. When I opened the front door, there were four of my friends all basically just wearing underwear, dressed up as bunnies and cats. I was full-on head-to-toe Wednesday Addams. I'd whited my face, drawn dark circles under my eyes, put my hair in pigtails, had a big white collar and was carrying a doll with its head taken off. I was like, 'Guys, come on!'

Harrison's taken my approach on board when they do Halloween Day at school because it really bugs him when people dress up as Cinderella or Spider-Man. He's like 'It's the Day of the Dead, people!' We put so much effort into their costumes each year, with Jude as Jack Skellington and Chucky the past couple of years and Harrison as Beetlejuice and Edward Scissorhands. It's become a bit of a thing now and the boys seem to enjoy it too, so I hope it's something they remember from their childhood as a special thing. If we ever have a Halloween Party (Covid has scuppered it for the past two years), I'm always Wednesday. Although this year, I did buy the red wedding dress costume that Winona Ryder wore as Lydia in *Beetlejuice*, and a few years ago I did go as Bride of Chucky.

I always wondered what I'd be like if I saw a ghost. And then one day I did. Although it was a ghost dog – does that count? I was about ten and staying over with my gran and papa. Sometimes if we were watching TV upstairs, they'd lay out a floor bed for me with my duvet and pillows on the carpet. One night, I was on the floor bed. The bedroom door was open which led on to a little landing with stairs going down, so if I raised my head I could see downstairs. That night I woke up in the middle of the night and realized I had to go to the toilet. I sat up and looked out into the hallway but it was pretty much pitch black so I wondered if I should wake my papa up to get him to turn the light on. But suddenly I saw this pair of glowing green eyes coming up the stairs towards me. I sat bolt upright and it got closer. It was a really big, dark (but not black) hairy dog with pointy ears, like a German shepherd, and it sat on the top of the stairs on the landing just looking at me with its bright green eyes. I could hear it softly breathing. I just stared at it and after a few seconds it got up, turned around really calmly and slowly, then started going back down the stairs. But then as it walked down the stairs, it just completely disappeared.

James always thinks that I must have been dreaming, but I swear to God, I wasn't. I went to the toilet afterwards! I remember sitting up for ages and then waking my papa up and telling him I thought there was a dog in the house. I wasn't scared, I just stared at it thinking, *Huh, why's there a dog there?* But then as I sat there looking at it, and it got up and turned around, I just knew it was a ghost. Something just didn't seem right about it. This story always comes up at Christmas and I tell it and James always shouts out 'She was dreaming!' I think it makes him feel better about it but I can still see the dog's face, clear as day!

My papa had all the time in the world for his grandkids. He was such a great papa and everyone loved him. He was just so easy-going, calm and cool. And sometimes, if I'm a bit stressed out, tired or if the kids are arguing or whatever and I find myself thinking, *Guys, come on!* then I get this really overwhelming thought about my papa, and he'd be saying, 'OK, what are they actually doing wrong? Nothing. You're annoyed because you're tired.' And whenever he'd hear one of the parents shushing their kids, he always used to say, 'What would you do if they never spoke again?' And someone would say, 'That'd be terrible!' So he'd reply with, 'So enjoy listening to them!' And when I hear that in my head, I take a breath and say, 'Guys, if we could just...' Or I hear him saying, 'Ah, careful, I did this for you, so don't be too hard on them.' It just feels like he's there because I hear his words so clearly. My boys never met him, sadly, but he's such an important figure in my life that they know all about him. It feels like they've got a relationship with him and that he's still here.

(From 'Hey Jude', by The Beatles, written by Lennon–McCartney)

I know the boys have been lucky with the people that have come into their lives, like Steve and Sally Cradock and our friends John and Clare. They're also very close to their cousins, aunts and uncles. My family is still close and so my cousins are now considered their aunts and uncles too. Sometimes they do get to enjoy experiences that other kids their age don't have as a result of James doing what he does. And part of the reason for that is because *The Inbetweeners* keeps appealing to people because it's kind of timeless. Every 16- or 17-year-old boy is in that kind of group and has those kinds of conversations, so the show stays relevant. And it keeps getting mentioned by people, for example like DanTDM (the massively successful YouTuber and gamer who almost every kid in the world knows). I remember the moment DanTDM said something about *The Inbetweeners* on his channel because I suddenly heard this wild screaming upstairs from the boys. When I went up to see what the hell had happened, it turns out that DanTDM had just said something about watching classic comedies like *Only Fools and Horses* and *The Inbetweeners*. The boys made me and James watch the bit where Dan mentioned the show, which he described as 'an old classic'. James was partly proud but you could also tell that his soul was being crushed slightly before he said, 'Jesus, I'm so old!'

Not long after that, because the boys were such big fans of Dan's, we bought them tickets for one of his live shows at the O2 in London. James sent Dan a message on Twitter to say that the boys were big fans and Dan said he'd love to say hi to them afterwards. When we told the boys, you should have seen their faces – they were nearly crying, they love the guy so much. They know they're very lucky when their dad can pull these sorts of strings.

 **James**: In early 2016, I mentioned on Twitter that I was thinking about starting a YouTube channel talking about and playing video games, and a whole load of people seemed to think it was a good idea. So, in April that year I started a channel called *Completed it Mate*. (I couldn't call it anything else really!) The very first video that I ever put up I shot on my camera phone and I was whispering and shaking with nerves. I had no idea what I was doing really. I've got an NES (with the gun, although it doesn't work on my TV), an SNES, a Mega Drive, an N64, an Xbox (which is what I store my TV remotes on), an Xbox 360, a PS1, PS2, PS3 (the twentieth

anniversary limited edition one) and an Atari 2600, which was the first games console that appeared one day in my house as a kid. It felt like playing arcades at home and that was an amazing feeling. It had *Pac-Man*, *Pong*, *Space Invaders*, all that stuff.

I know this sounds dramatic but my first memory of being alive was playing *Smurf: Rescue in Gargamel's Castle* on the Atari 2600. I must have been barely three and I was plonked down in the living room in front of the TV and left to get on with it, like so many kids who grew up when I did! And I think we've all realized that's probably not the healthiest way to bring up a kid, however much they love it. But in my parents' defence, I was perfectly happy, so I can understand not wanting to bother me. I got used to controlling a dot or a square on a TV screen and you'd have to use your imagination to turn it into what it was actually supposed to be, like a bat or a tank. But with the Smurfs game, you could make out that it was a Smurf (it was blue and white and had a hat on and everything). But when I saw Sonic the Hedgehog's face on the Sega Master System, it was another of those 'Right, this is it!' moments, where you wonder how things can get any better. Nothing else mattered any more. (I can hear Clair saying 'You're so dramatic!' when I say that out loud.) Sonic just took me to places I wanted to get to. And that's why I play video games. Plus, on the Master System, some of the games came built in as well so you didn't need to buy the cartridge. What a time to be alive! Some of the sounds from those consoles are so evocative.

Harrison and Jude have got toys that make the noise of Sonic collecting a ring and the question mark on *Super Mario*. I can hear it even if it's barely audible, I'm just so tuned into it.

When I was on my Atari 2600, though, every other kid was playing the NES (Nintendo Entertainment System), the Super Nintendo or the Sega Mega Drive. When my mates were playing with their Mega Drives, we'd have a second-hand Sega Master System. We were always one step behind on the console front, and I remember getting a Mega Drive just as the Sony PlayStation came out. But also, I was lucky enough that I grew up in a time when you spent a lot of time at friends' houses, so I never really missed out. But in hindsight, I grew up with the previous generation's video games, which were still amazing and brilliant and I didn't appreciate at the time all the good things that brought with it. Now I very much do and feel like I have an extra helping of nostalgia that I can enjoy.

The console always had to be put away after we'd finished playing with it and the TV aerial plugged back in. Eventually your RF cable would start to get a bit wiggly and you'd have to start bending it, then sellotaping it to the console to get it in the right position. Those days are long gone. Now you can plug about twelve HDMI cables into one TV and you're away.

If I could play one video game for the rest of my life, it would probably be multiplayer *GoldenEye*. I remember seeing it on someone's TV for the first time and thinking, *This is it! How can you ever make a video game look better than this? That looks like Pierce Brosnan and Sean Bean! We've reached the pinnacle of human achievement.* And then you go back and play it again and you think, *What's all this smudge that I'm looking at? I can't make out anything.* I got the N64 in 1998 (it came out in the UK in spring 1997) and I was acting in *Whistle Down the Wind* at the Aldwych Theatre. And a Game Boy for the first time, which made me look forward to those Tube journeys on the way to the theatre. It was absolutely brilliant. I got it when the Pokémon games were just starting to come out, which were amazing.

I love the Mega Drive so much. The Sonic games got even better and they looked more and more amazing. And games like *ToeJam & Earl* just blew my mind. They just delved ever so slightly deeper than the massively popular ones. Whenever I hear anything even vaguely close to the theme tune, it takes me back to *ToeJam*. Apparently the designer originally called it 'Flow Jam and Whirl' but there was a mix-up with the programmer who wrote it down as 'ToeJam and Earl' and Sega ended up really liking the name. The intro music on that game is like an anthem of my childhood. A bit like the opening monologue to *SuperTed*, which I still know word for word.

On the Mega Drive, Disney brought out some amazing games like *The Lion King*, *The Jungle Book* and *Aladdin*. *Toy Story* on the Mega Drive is absolutely brilliant and it actually has a level where you're in first person playing Buzz trying to get out of the amusement park claw game thing. *Road Rash* and *Road Rash II* are just incredible games. Quite violent for back then, though, allowing you to race motorbikes, nick weapons off other characters and police officers and then smash them off their bikes with the bat or chain you've stolen from them. What made anyone think that was all right for kids to play was mental, but what a game!

Golden Axe was another great game, which still holds up now. You'd have three characters to choose from, and everyone would go for the dwarf, because he was the best, but sometimes I'd go for the hot lady. She was so sexy and confusing to an eight-year-old boy. I remember just staring at the cover of the game. *Golden Axe II* was even better – what a classic.

Ecco the Dolphin was completely groundbreaking. I remember my mate had it on the Sega Game Gear. I think I'm still recovering from the first time I saw a Game Gear. My tiny little mind was just destroyed. I could not believe what I was seeing, backlit, with all the colours and you could hold it and take it around with you. It was just so expensive though. One of my cousins brought one along to the reception at a wedding we all went to when we were young. Our parents were all getting pissed and we were really bored, but then he whipped out this Game Gear and all the kids crowded round watching and waiting their turn. We had the time of our lives!

I wasn't old enough to experience the cultural phenomenon of kids all meeting up in the arcade, unless it was at a caravan park or you were at the seaside. There was never one on the high street that you could hang out at.

It's still huge in Japan, the arcade culture where kids will buy a Coke and spend the afternoon playing games with their mates.

As a teenager, *Age of Empires II* was the first game that I played online and me and mates would wait until 6pm when the Internet didn't cost a fortune, unplug the phone and plug our PCs in and play *Age of Empires II* for hours. We told each other that we'd meet in 'Aging Cor' because we didn't understand what Agincourt was then. Even though the graphics have all changed on games and they're now all super-sharp, nothing can replace the nostalgia value of playing old games with their original dodgy graphics. And there's still a market for creating games that look like that. If the game's good, it'll always be a fun game.

I didn't have a PC growing up as a young kid and neither did any of my mates, it was all consoles. I didn't really understand playing games on PCs until much later. I was always struggling with the keyboard and the mouse. Video game controllers are made specifically so you can play video games but trying to adapt something that was designed to write a letter and draw up spreadsheets into a controller is always going to cause problems. All the PC 'games' I came across in my teens were educational ones that you'd see on the computers at school, like Microsoft *Encarta*, where you definitely wouldn't be smacking people off with a chain.

My Favourite Video Game

Grand Theft Auto: Vice City is my favourite game of all time. I wouldn't go as far as to say it's the best game of all time though, because it's all subjective. But it's my favourite because: one – it's just a really good game; and two – it came out on the PlayStation 2. The PS2 was an incredible console – the bestselling console of all time in fact, with over 150 million of them flying off the shelves. And I think one of the reasons it did so well is because they made a genius decision to make it a DVD player as well, and it was cheaper than most DVD players at the time, so lots of families bought one because it killed two birds with one stone.

I was 15 when *GTA: Vice City* came out in 2002 and I was massively into video games, as were all my friends. It was the game everyone talked about. And for good reason because I loved the music, characters, cut scenes, voice acting (you've got Ray Liotta, Burt Reynolds, Tom Sizemore, Luis Guzmán and my mate Danny Dyer), and the story's amazing. It's also very funny. There are loads of in-jokes and it's a great send-up of all of those gangster films. The writing is so good too. It's such an immersive game that you get completely lost in it and so much fun. It looks incredible and the cars are cool. Yeah, there are better games technically but it doesn't matter – this one will always be my favourite.

I've even got the seven-CD boxset, which has all the music from the different radio stations you listen to in your car in the game. I love that you always end up with your favourite radio station in the game – mine was Wave 103, which was new wave and synthpop stuff from the 1980s like The Human League, Blondie and Frankie Goes to Hollywood. And the other songs on the other stations you listen to a fair bit too and they just stick with you so you forever associate them with the joy of playing that game. Sometimes a song will come on the radio when you're listening to Absolute 80s and I'll wonder why I'm suddenly taking notice of it so much but then it hits you: it's on *GTA: Vice City*.

I've gone through story mode so many times and on different devices now, too, like the iPad. It's just a completely iconic game. *GTA III* was great when that came out in 2001, they'd taken the brand and the franchise and moved it on so much from that sort of bird's-eye view, top-down style to the sandboxy, third-person angle. The artwork of *GTA* is amazing, with its cartoony, comic-book style, which might have been all that was really available at the time, but they set the game in the 1980s anyway, so it all works perfectly and captures a moment in time.

I've only got one criticism of *Vice City* and that's the fact you've got such a hard mission early on in the game using the remote-controlled helicopter to blow up the construction site. I thought it was impossible after trying it a few times, but you eventually get the hang of the controls, and when you finally complete it, oh my God, what a relief that is. I like to think that I could do it first time now even though I haven't played it for years.

Super Mario Kart on the Super Nintendo is still one of the best ways to spend an afternoon with a mate or with Clair and the boys, and if you get the controller expansion pack you can plug four of them in and play battle mode, where you have to burst each other's balloons. A few beers and that's party time! I still play *The Legend of Zelda* a lot on the SNES too.

Gaming used to be a solitary thing where you'd lock yourself away and not talk to anyone for hours, sometimes days, until you'd completed the game, but it's become so social and I love that attitudes have changed like that. It's great that we're all connected doing something we love. I've been lucky enough to meet professional gamers like Callum 'Swanny' Swan, a then-pro *Call of Duty* player. I'm not, and never have been, that good at computer games but I love playing them.

What I've always said about my relationship with video games is that friends have come and gone and Clair might get fed up with me one day, but I'll always have games. It's the one constant relationship that I know for sure that I'm guaranteed to have for my whole life.

I'm quite an anxious person, but when I'm in front of a camera and I'm playing a part, I find that quite easy. But ask me to sit down and be myself, I find that really nerve-wracking. And I'm still always slightly nervous when I'm making a YouTube video but I feel like I've overcome that anxiety a bit and become more comfortable in myself. One of the ways in which I felt like I'd turned a corner with my social anxiety was back in 2017 on *The Graham Norton Show* when I basically told the whole nation that I'd shat my pants (look out for that anecdote in The Art of the Fart on page 206). If you notice, in interviews with the four of us *Inbetweeners* boys I was always sitting in the corner or in the back and tended to rely on the other three, who are more likeable and funnier than me, to get me through the interview and I'd hardly say a word. But now I feel more comfortable doing those things and talking to people. It's something that YouTube has really helped me with. I feel a lot happier in my own skin. It helps that 99.9 per cent of the comments on our YouTube channel are supportive. I honestly like reading comments.

I started my YouTube channel *Completed it Mate* because I wanted to find out more about filming, directing, editing and creating my own content. As an actor, it's great being told what to do all the time – and people think you're brilliant and very funny – but there's a part of me that wants to be more involved in creating content and YouTube felt like a really good way for me to go out and do little videos about anything I wanted and just learn the basics of putting together videos. Plus, it's really fun and I enjoy it. The first few videos I shot on my phone and they were really bad, but the people who watched them were very helpful suggesting which equipment and software to buy. I now find it quite therapeutic doing YouTube videos.

James on Bond

I love my Bond films and Timothy Dalton's the best Bond for me, because he's bloody brilliant. First and foremost, he's very underrated. Anyone that's a true Bond fan appreciates what Dalton brought to the character, especially after the sort of slapsticky Roger Moore, and Jaws just turning up in lots of films and falling in love with the tiny woman in space. Also, there was a big gap because of the dispute between EON and MGM, so the first Bond films I watched when I was five or six were the Dalton ones. But as I've grown older, I still really appreciate him. I love *Licence to Kill* – that's my favourite Bond film, and *The Living Daylights* is great as well. When you listen to his interviews from around the time he was filming them, he talks about how Bond is an assassin, a calculated killer. He's almost like a robot, trained to do a job which he's very good at, and that's how he thinks. Those two films are a lot more serious than the others just before it. I think Dalton swears properly as well, and you never really hear that.

I've got a theory that there are two types of Bond. You've got the Sean Connery type and the Roger Moore type. And the producers switch. First, you've got Sean Connery, who's your classic rough and tough, get the job done, no mucking about. Then you've got Roger Moore, who's more suave, handsome and all about little quips. Then with Dalton, you're back to more of the no-nonsense agent, before Pierce Brosnan takes over with a return to the slick, witty charmer. And then you've got Daniel Craig, another focused, no messing tough guy. So I think we're due a bit of fun next and that's what the world needs right now, so I'm up for a Roger Moore-style, one-liner type of Bond. It would put a smile on everyone's face.

I've seen the latest one, *No Time to Die*, and it's a good film, but it's not what I'm after in a Bond if I'm honest. It goes against everything Bond should be in my opinion. I do really like Daniel Craig, though. When I was thinking about what I wanted to do for a living, I was obsessed with British films and British actors, and one of my favourite films was *The Trench*, a film about a bunch of young British soldiers about to go over the top on the first day of the Battle of the Somme. Daniel Craig plays the tough sergeant and loads of other British actors are in it, like Danny Dyer and Ben Whishaw. I remember him in *Layer Cake* as well.

Being in front of the camera as an actor I sort of go on autopilot because the words and jokes are written for me and I just have to deliver them. It's almost like I have a manual telling me what to do and a director, producer and writer all doing this and that. I think a lot of actors are like that though. We tend to be quite nervous, insecure, shy and not very confident people. And maybe they pick acting as a career to make up for that. And that might have been part of the reason I became an actor.

 **Clair**: In *The Comedian's Guide to Survival* (2016), James was playing the comedian James Mullinger (who co-wrote the script based on his own life). The producers wanted James to do the film and he just thought it was one of those things that he couldn't turn down. He'd been used to being in an ensemble cast so this was his first big project where he was literally in every scene and he had to work really hard to drive it. I ended up playing his wife and to be fair it was a good fit, because his wife needed to seem really fed up and pissed off with him, so I wouldn't really call it acting, to be honest! I'd done a little bit of acting in this and that but once I'd had my babies, I was happy doing the mum thing. But this sounded fun, so I asked my mum to come down and look after the boys and I went off in the daytime (the location wasn't that far from us) for a couple of days to shoot the scenes.

One of the things I had to do was throw a saucepan at

James, but luckily for him, it was Styrofoam. But man, oh man, I could not throw that thing straight. It had to hit him on the head, that was the whole point, but every time I threw it, it just sailed on by. So that scene took forever. You feel all this pressure because there are so many people on set who just want to go home at a decent time and if you keep messing things up, you're stopping this from happening. So I ended up apologizing to everyone a lot. I'm not good at small talk, and nor is James for that matter. I'm sure everyone we meet thinks we're arseholes, but we're actually just a bit socially awkward. Maybe we just don't spend enough time with other people. We're OK at home, and I think that's why the vlog works, but as soon as another person turns up, we panic.

I was in *Vendetta* in 2013, an action film starring our mate Danny Dyer, who James has known since he was about 18. It was actually the first film I'd been in, and I played the high-profile role of 'New York City victim'. It was a last-minute thing where Danny asked if I wanted to play a little part and then we'd catch up and go for a pint afterwards, although I was pregnant with Jude at the time, so James and Danny did the drinking. It was good to do a bit of acting, though, and Danny knew I wanted to dip my toes back into it. Sometimes James and I do get invited to premieres, screenings and things like that, but we tend to leave when people start mentioning clubs. We'll head home, grab a McDonald's on the way and stick *Bob's Burgers* on in bed. But to be fair, we're parents, so we've gotta head back. We're not big after-party people. James and I showed Harrison and Jude the scene I was in from *Vendetta* but Jude hated it because my character gets mugged. Because I'm pregnant in the scene, I was telling the boys that Jude had been in a film and Harrison was like 'No he hasn't!'

The last film I was in was *Monster*, which came out in 2018. My agent got me an audition at the BBC in London but I had to put on an English accent, which I was terrified about. The character was someone who says a little bit and then gets murdered. I thought my audition went horribly but after a couple of days they called my agent and said they really liked it and wanted me to come back in. I wore a little Guns N' Roses tank top and I think that, combined with my tattoos, made them think about me for a different role to the one I auditioned for. It was a slightly bitchy girl with a really bad attitude and they were happy for me to keep my normal accent. That all sounded cool, but to be honest, as a massive horror fan, I was annoyed that my new character didn't get murdered!

When I arrived to film it, I might have told a few people on set that I was a bit gutted not to be murdered. And then a couple of days later, the director took me aside and said, 'Clair – we're going to kill you. I think we've got time.' I was so happy. I would love to exclusively act in horror films, ideally getting murdered, or maybe even being the murderer, but it doesn't really work that way. Before I did *Monster*, I acted in a little student film and that was the first time I'd done horror, but it was so much fun. To be honest, even if I saw the script and knew it was terrible, I love horror so much that I'd probably do it. James loves horror films, but in a completely different way.

Fart Attacks

People have been complaining that I haven't been farting enough in recent vlogs so I'm taking you back to that magical time in our second vlog where Clair got the hump about a trump.

Clair: I'm so sick of this! Does that one stink?

James: No it doesn't stink. And do you know what? You're hurting my feelings a little bit.

Clair: Oh shut up!

James: Sometimes you accidentally do a little fart and you want to move on from it and you feel embarrassed.

Clair: But you don't feel embarrassed!

James: That was an accident!

Clair: You're sitting there with your legs open and you're letting it all out. It's disgusting.

James: I'm embarrassed. And you kept all those farts in from the first vlog and I am mortified. I was really hoping that you wouldn't do that to me. You made me look a fool. And I've never looked a fool on television before.

Clair: People might be watching this when they're eating!

James: Then I apologize. I'm sorry. But you fart a lot as well and no one has a go at you for it.

Clair: I don't fart a lot. And even when I do, mine don't stink out a whole room. If you do it again, you're in trouble.

James: No, I'm telling you, I think there's something going on. I think I'm hungry. I need a drink. Has it gone midday yet?

James: I get a weirdly strange pleasure from being scared. I don't know why but it's almost addictive because I know I'm not going to like it but I really want more of it. You've got to go to the cinema to see a horror film, with the big screen in the pitch black and the huge speakers, for the full effect. Although I'll get scared anywhere to be honest, including on set when I was in *The Pyramid* (2014), a horror film about an archaeological team who find a pyramid buried beneath the desert. We filmed it in a place called Ouarzazate in Morocco, nicknamed 'the door to the desert' as it's a stopover on the way to the Sahara. It's not a big place – there's literally a film studio, a couple of hotels and a French restaurant. But the studio was the one where they shot parts of *Gladiator*, *The Mummy* and one of my favourite Bond movies, *The Living Daylights*, which was pretty cool.

What wasn't so cool was the journey to the studio. My flight got cancelled and then when I finally got to Ouarzazate and got picked up from the airport, one of the car's tyres blew out in the middle of the desert road we were driving up. It got to the point that it felt like someone was trying to stop me from actually turning up. To be fair, though, there have been quite a few horror films where things go wrong. *The Exorcist*, for one. There were all these stories of people fainting in the cinema and stuff, and most of that was a kind of marketing gimmick. But two of the actors did actually die before the film was released. On set Ellen Burstyn (who played Regan's mum) and Linda Blair (who played Regan) both suffered spinal injuries. And a bird flew into a circuit box on the set of Regan's house, starting a massive fire. Weirdly, the only part of the set to survive was the bedroom where the exorcism actually happens. Apparently they ended up calling in a priest to bless the set!

The next thing I think I worked on after *The Pyramid* was a TV series in 2016 made by Baby Cow, the production company co-founded by Steve Coogan, who I've already fanboyed about. It was a sitcom called *Zapped*, an original scripted comedy series commissioned by Dave (it might have been their first one), and it was set almost entirely in the fantasy world of Munty. Most of the action takes place in a pub called The Jug and the Other Jug, where my character Brian becomes trapped after being transported there when he puts on a magical amulet.

Zapped was a special one for lots of reasons, one of which was working with Paul Kaye again, who I'd first met on the film *The Comedian's Guide to Survival*. I read the script for that film and really liked it but asked the producers who else was going to be in it. They told me they were in talks with Paul Kaye, and I basically said if he was going to be in it, I'd do it because I'd wanted to act with him for ages. I grew up watching him as Dennis Pennis and being inspired by the kind of amazing roles he made his own.

With *Zapped*, I got the pilot script from my agent and, unusually, it was three episodes, which I really like because it gives you a proper opportunity to show what the show's about, as opposed to a single 22-minute transmission, which never feels like enough. So it was really great that Dave supported the project like that and gave it a chance. And to their huge credit, they were like that the whole way through. And it was a bizarre idea for a show too. What I liked about it more than anything was the parallel between it and *Red Dwarf*. It was basically set in a pub in an alternate universe where everyone looks like they're on the set of *Game of Thrones*. But even though I liked the script, I doubted myself because of the nature of the role. I wasn't sure if I'd have as much fun as the lead character in the way that I'd done in ensemble comedies like *The Inbetweeners* or something like *White Gold* (which started a bit later than *Zapped*) where there is a lead but I get to come on and be funny. That's the area I like to operate in, so this was way outside my comfort zone.

To be honest, after doing *The Comedian's Guide to Survival* I wasn't really sure if I had the chops to be the focal point of a project. I wasn't confident that I was actually good enough an actor to drive it. So I turned down *Zapped*. Then they asked me if I'd reconsider, which was flattering, but I said no again. I honestly thought there were people out there who could do a better job than me. Some time later, I got a call from my agent who told me that the director, producer and Steve Coogan wanted to meet me for lunch and talk about it. I thought it would be one of those situations where I'd turn up for lunch and the director and producer would be there and apologize that

Steve couldn't make it but would tell me that they really wanted to talk to me about the show. But I turned up and there was Steve, shaking my hand.

I don't think I'd made it a secret of how much of a Steve Coogan fan I am and how much of a hero he is to me. I think what happened is that the producers of *Zapped* told him that if he had a meeting with me, I'd take the part. And if that was their plan, it worked perfectly.

I sat there staring at Steve in disbelief because I couldn't believe he'd turned up. And after about five minutes, he turned to me and said, 'I think you'd be really good in *Zapped* and I'd really like you to do it.' And I said, 'Well yeah, I'll do it! Did someone say I wouldn't do it?! Ha ha – this has all been a big misunderstanding, Steve, of course I'm going to do it!' It felt a little bit like a meeting where Don Corleone would turn up, look you intensely in the eyes and say 'Some wiseguy's told me you're not going to do this.' And you panic and say, 'Oh no, sir, I'm your man! When do we start?!' But I'm really glad I got to do *Zapped* and I was so pleased that a lot of people loved the show, unfortunately just not enough for us to carry on beyond series three. We left it on a cliffhanger because we thought we were going to go again for another series, because even though it wasn't getting huge numbers, for original scripted content on Dave it was doing very well. It cost quite a lot to make, though, because it was set in a fantasy world that they had to create from scratch. It's never nice having something cancelled because you can't help but feel as though you've failed and you're left thinking, *I wish we could have had one more go at this*, which is how I felt then. I'm glad we got three series, though. I really don't like it when a series gets cancelled after one full series because it usually takes that long to understand properly what works. Dave gave it a good shot, though, and got behind it more than I think any other network would have done.

Baby Cow was also producing another series at the time, which was, like *Zapped*, being shot at Pinewood Studios. It was a little-known show called *Red Dwarf* (Baby Cow did series XI and XII). They filmed the two series back to back, mainly because the four guys were worried about looking old, so wanted to get on with it, but the transmission dates were staggered between 2015 and 2016.

Red Dwarf is one of my favourite ever shows, so much so that I watch it all the way through each year when I arrive in Los Angeles for pilot season. They started filming the first series of *Red Dwarf* the year I was born (1987) and I literally can't remember my life before that iconic show.

In 2017 I was asked by the show's creator if I wanted to be in an episode. I agreed. I didn't even try to play it cool. I think I said yes midway through the actual question. They told me I'd play an alien or something like that so no one would recognize me, which I thought sounded cool. I couldn't believe my luck really.

It was only about a week before we were due to shoot the episode, when I was having a make-up test done, that I actually found out what they wanted me to do, which was to play an android that looked like Kryten. And all of a sudden I got incredibly nervous because Kryten is such an iconic look. I didn't want to play my character – Rusty – like Kryten, though. I thought the comedy would come from me looking like Kryten but having an East End sort of accent and saying the sort of things you'd expect to hear in a pub. And the producers and the *Red Dwarf* boys were up for me messing about and having a bit of fun with the script, which was amazing. I really like that juxtaposition of characters who look like they're from a fantasy or science-fiction world but their behaviour is completely grounded in the real world.

After the series was shot, the *Red Dwarf* boys personally asked for me to interview them for the *Red Dwarf* series release promo. So I turned up, having written all the interview questions myself, which was probably the right way to go seeing as I wanted to ask things that fans wanted to know. The four of them were all absolutely brilliant, amazingly funny and genuinely interesting people, all with a tale to tell. I could have stayed there all day. Actually, I think I did in the end.

One of my favourite programmes in that kind of style is the animated *God, the Devil and Bob*, which ran in 2000 for just one series, starring James Garner as God, Alan Cumming as the Devil, French Stewart as Bob, Laurie Metcalf as Bob's wife and Nancy Cartwright (the voice of Bart Simpson) as their daughter. And the Devil and God are just regular guys who have a beer and a chat and talk through the administration of running hell. I love the fact that the Devil is any old geezer really, but he just happens to find himself running hell. I would keep telling people about that series and I remember no one ever knew what I was going on about, until I met Clair! Which was unbelievable. She actually mentioned it to me one evening, saying something like, 'Oh, there was a cartoon I used to watch all the time about God and the Devil and a wee guy.' (She couldn't remember the name.) I shouted, '*God, the Devil and Bob!*' She was like, 'Yeah, that's it.'

Red Dwarf does everything I want from a sitcom. It's a pub comedy really, but it's set in space. You've got four ridiculous people – the last man from Earth, a hologram of the person he had the most interaction with on the ship created to keep him sane (but unfortunately the person he had the most interaction with on the ship was the one he hated the most), a cat that evolved over millions of years to become humanoid and an android that they find in a crashed ship on a planet. The performances and the characters are so fully formed and all so completely relatable, and in many ways it's a very traditional sitcom but for the fact that they're marooned in space in the future. There's something funny every 30 seconds and it's just brilliant. And it doesn't matter that everything basically takes place in one of three places: the cockpit, the crew's quarters and the canteen. Every now and then they might push the boat out and go to a planet or a loading bay, but the limited sets just add the kind of claustrophobic intensity that can make a sitcom so good.

Similar to *Only Fools and Horses*, in *Red Dwarf* you've got characters who all have their little wins and losses. Even though Rimmer as a person (well, hologram) is just an absolute cock, there are a handful of occasions where he does the most heroic stuff that briefly redeems him. There's a glimmer of Rimmer not being a complete slimeball all the time. And the writing and acting is brilliant because as a viewer, you don't completely hate the guy. You laugh at him, enjoy his quirks and even celebrate the glee that he feels when he gets one up on Lister in his petty way. He's weirdly likeable. I think it's rare for a sitcom to work when you haven't got likeable characters, though, apart from *It's Always Sunny in Philadelphia*, which has the genius idea of making sure you hate everyone just about equally. In that show, all the characters are just the worst people on the planet. They're all disgusting, narcissistic, ignorant and oblivious to it, but they are so much fun to watch. And I think part of the reason it works is because they never win, the joke is always on them, their lives are so sad and pathetic even though they probably think they're really successful and winning at life. That is the one sitcom that bucks the trend of having likeable characters. And it's a classic.

Talking of classics, I still can't quite believe my luck being in both *Red Dwarf* and the prequel to *Only Fools and Horses*. I've just got to pray that there's a *Blackadder* special at some point that I can wangle into and that's the full set. I was also in an episode of *The Comic Strip Presents...*, which was an amazing series, starring Rik Mayall, Adrian Edmondson, Dawn French, Jennifer Saunders and Nigel Planer among others. That was around about 2011 and that was insane being around such legends.

Ending up in this sort of situation, where I'm starring

in classic sitcoms and making a guest appearance in *Red Dwarf* and meeting all the guys isn't something I take for granted. I still have to remind myself that I did these things, not because I'm in danger of forgetting them, but because I can't believe I was lucky enough to have experienced them. Meeting Nicholas Lyndhurst, having lunch with David Jason and John Sullivan, these are all things that I'm not cool about, pretending that it's 'just another day at the office'. I still look back wondering how these things all came about. There's a lot of those self-help-type books that tell you if you picture something really clearly in your mind and pursue it, that it eventually does manifest. Well, it feels like exactly that sort of thing has happened in my career. Whether or not it's a coincidence or whether things have worked out because I've subconsciously positioned myself in the right sort of situations, I don't know, but it's also probably why I haven't been as successful as I could have been, perhaps, after *The Inbetweeners*. I've never been obsessed with being a household name and it's never been something that's fuelled me. So, I've never consciously sought that.

A guest slot on another classic series – *Doctor Who* – came along at a funny time, though, when I was a little bit older (it was 2019) and maybe not taking myself as seriously. I'd come out of a phase in my twenties of being quite driven and knowing what I wanted to do, and suddenly I found myself less interested in impressing people. I was just up for having more fun, but *Doctor Who* was so much hard work. I think the guys that make it are the hardest-working people in British television. I don't know how they do it. They essentially make ten or eleven mini films over the course of a few weeks to a high spec but on a relatively small budget. It's a miracle really. Everyone's so focused but they're up against it and the pressure is pretty intense. And that's not why I became an actor. If I wanted to work for a living I would have got a proper job! Also I thought I'd need to be in for like two days tops, but *Doctor Who* went on for ages. I ended up in the Canary Islands shooting some of it and just thinking, *This is a bit nuts*, particularly because I wasn't expecting to be flying abroad for it!

To be fair, though, I'd never watched an episode of *Doctor Who* so the whole thing was probably my fault, and maybe I shouldn't have agreed to do it. When we were shooting, I'd be running away from aliens and improvising with things like 'Help us, Doctor Who!' without realizing that you never actually say 'Doctor Who' – he or she is just 'the Doctor'. Bradley Walsh was in the show at that point, though, as the Doctor's companion and he was great. An absolute gent, I was so impressed with him – what a lovely bloke. I had been in an ITV drama with him years ago (I was about 16) and I had a very small part but I don't think I actually met him until I was on the set of *Doctor Who*.

Soon after I was saying yes to 'Don Corleone' Coogan and *Zapped*, Damon Beesley (co-creator of *The Inbetweeners*) got the go-ahead to make a series called *White Gold*. He'd actually told me and Joe about the idea for *White Gold* when we were making the first series of *The Inbetweeners* but it takes them a while to get round to doing stuff. I bet I'll see them making something in the next couple of years that I remember them talking about ages ago! But *White Gold* kind of made sense for me and Joe, given that both of us had grown up in Essex where it's set, and, well, we're both people that Damon likes. I think it was an excuse for us to work together again, which is always great. But what I absolutely loved about it was that it was a genuine representation of the 1980s instead of a romanticized, nostalgic look at that era. We could have gone for a super-cool look, but instead I modelled myself on eighties footballer Mark Lawrenson. I actually took pictures of him to hair and make-up – he was my inspiration and, to be fair to him, he stayed true to that look for years before eventually getting rid of the moustache. But that sort of weird blow-dried, where does your parting begin? kind of look from back in his Liverpool days was perfect. And Damon thought that was a good shout too. I wondered about going for a more slick, George Michael, yuppy cool, but I don't think you should try and be cool if you're trying to be funny. I think I need to look like a tit so that people can laugh at me. I've always said that.

My goal is usually to try and make people laugh and if you're dressed the part before you've even opened your mouth, you're already one step ahead. I take that mentality into every job I do in comedy. People can always say no if you go into a show with these kind of ideas but I've found most people are receptive to having a discussion about it. I got a bit more confident and creative after watching and working with Steve Coogan. And I've also got a bit older too and don't care as much what people think if I look like a tit. Unless I'm trying to look like a tit for comic effect of course.

James's Vinyl Collection Must-haves

Clair: I've just seen your *Desert Island Disc* choices. You went all romantic and meaningful with your list.

James: Yeah, I tried to avoid picking songs just 'because I like it'.

Clair: Oh, that's what all mine are!

James: I appreciated that we were trying to make a book, you see, and people might want to read something interesting.

Clair: They've come to the wrong place then!

James: Do you remember that vlog we did when we were sitting down by the record player and talking about albums that you have to have in your vinyl collection?

Clair: God, what do we sound like?!

James: We're vloggers now, Clair. That's the kind of thing vloggers do, isn't it?

Clair: How should I know?

James: People went mental for that vlog.

Clair: Who did?

James: You know, the...people. So due to unprece-dented public demand, I've written a list of must-have albums. So these are albums that basically make you look like a normal, respectable person who has some music taste.

Clair: But that's pointless!

James: It's all pointless Clair!

Clair: Yeah but my must-haves are ones that I *must have*. I like what I like and I know what I like and that's all I need. When we first started going out, you'd try and introduce me to songs that I'd never heard of and you couldn't believe it. But I didn't need another song. I've already got all my songs.

James: You can't just listen to six bands for the rest of your life!

Clair: Look Jimmy, I'd quite happily just listen to The Beatles for three months solid, then switch to The Jam for three months and keep spending the rest of my life rotating. But I do like some recent bands. The Kooks – they're a new, hip, happening band, aren't they?!

James: Their first album came out in 2006!

Clair: That's recent, isn't it? Look, *Inside In/Inside Out* is top-notch. And I did like Arctic Monkeys' first album *Whatever People Say I Am, That's What I'm Not*. That's insanely good.

James: Also 2006.

Clair: I love an album you don't have to skip anything on. That would be a better list of albums.

James: Look – I'm just trying to look the part and trick people into thinking 'Maybe this guy knows something about something.' And full disclosure, I have actually listened to all except one of these albums, but I'm not telling you the one I haven't heard all the way through. And if someone quizzes me about that one, I'll make sure to keep my comments about it short and ambiguous. 'What an album that is – iconic. Groundbreaking. Ahead of its time.' That sort of thing. Then I can pass for someone who might know what they're talking about.

Clair: You actors, eh?!

James: So I'm going for *The Stone Roses* by The Stone Roses. You can see the cover in your head immediately.

Clair: OK, that is a great album.

James: So the next one is *What's Going On* by Marvin Gaye, then *Dark Side of the Moon* by Pink Floyd. Got to have it, great album, amazing cover, get it on your shelf.

Clair: I've never listened to that one all the way through.

James: Yes you have, it's been on of an afternoon. You weren't paying attention. Next one: *Appetite for Destruction* by Guns N' Roses.

Clair: I'll give you that.

James: Next one up: *Rumours* by Fleetwood Mac.

Clair: Love that one too.

James: The next three are *Pet Sounds* by The Beach Boys, *The Doors* by The Doors, *Nevermind* by Nirvana. Then I went for *The Rise and Fall of Ziggy Stardust and the Spiders From Mars* by David Bowie. That feels like the most iconic Bowie album and you can instantly see the cover of the album in your head.

Clair: Agreed.

James: Now I'm not a massive Joy Division fan, I like maybe three of their songs, but for respectability purposes, when it comes to the influence they've had, you have to have them on your list. Now, no one's brave enough to say that Joy Division are overrated. Including me. Except they are. So I've got their debut album *Unknown Pleasures* on the list. And the last one is *Revolver* by The Beatles. Got to have one Beatles album in there.

Clair: Just one?!

[James flees area.]

5

Clair: We decided to do the vlog just before lockdown in 2020. I remember James and I talking about how we didn't seem to do anything any more, compared with years ago when we'd go to gigs, living our little rock 'n' roll life, and bring the boys along. We got them little ear defenders and we'd rock away, sometimes going away for the weekend and coming back on the Monday night. But as the kids got older and started school, we just didn't have the time to do those kinds of things. It got to a point in the last couple of years, when the kids were about eight and six that we just got a bit comfortable in our house, stopped going out and stopped meeting new people. While that was fine for that time in life, as the kids were getting older and had their own social lives (kids' parties are constant!) I just felt like James and I had to get some life back into us! We are still young and should be taking advantage of that!

So we decided that we needed to shake things up a bit. James thought starting a vlogging channel was a great idea, something we could do together, and he wasn't getting any work at that point so figured we should give it a go because it might encourage us to go out, see stuff and do stuff because you need content! We also had bills to pay, so a vlog channel where we could maybe be lucky enough to have sponsorships could hit two birds with one stone! But then lockdown came along and the vlog sort of became us in our house messing about. And I know people enjoy that. But since things have opened up, we're doing a lot more. The vlog has really helped us. It's as much for us as it is for the people who watch it. Of course, it takes some work to get the vlogs ready and up on YouTube so it's always great when we get a sponsor for a video. When you're putting work into something, it's nice when your work results in a payment. Just like most jobs do. But it's definitely not why we do it…obviously, I mean we rarely have a sponsor, ha ha! It's made us work together and that was the first time we'd ever really worked together. And if one of us is not feeling it, the other will be the driving force. Even if it's just going outside and doing a bit of gardening or starting silly conversations about cereal or crisps.

Crisps

Clair: We both love a packet of crisps. They take us back to our childhoods when you'd stop by the newsagent with whatever cash you'd scraped together and go to town on the 10p crisps. When we talk about crisps now, James starts getting all technical and theatrical about them, describing them in terms of moisture content and surface area, but he's like that. He's an overthinker. So, for your amusement, I thought I'd share with you a conversation James and I had that we vlogged but it didn't make the cut. It started, as all good chats do, when I opened a bag of pickled onion Monster Munch. Because we're all about the highbrow content as you know.

Clair: You know what – pickled onion Monster Munch are top tier crisps.

James: They're up there. Do you remember they brought out a version of pickled onion flavour that made your tongue turn blue?

Clair: Yeah, that was a Halloween special.

James: Of course you'd know that.

Clair: Remember they had green ketchup for a while? And I'll tell you what, roast beef Monster Munch are so underrated. I remember when it came back after it disappeared for a few years. What a day that was.

James: True. And you know what Monster Munch do well? There aren't any album fillers. If you get a multipack of Walkers, you'll always end up with the ready salted ones left. And you eventually eat them, because, you know, they're crisps, but you're not happy about it. But with Monster Munch, there'll be nothing left in that multipack. If someone said to me, 'I'm going to get some Monster Munch from the kitchen, what flavour do you want?' I'd say, You pick. Treat yourself.' Because you can't go wrong.

Clair: Apart from Monster Munch though, the best ones were all 10p. Oinks, Spicy Bikers, Tangy Toms…

James: Do you remember when I nearly choked on a Tangy Tom?

Clair: So I found Tangy Toms in Aldi last year. James was so excited when he got back home. And of course, put the whole packet in his mouth. But one got properly stuck and it suddenly became a scene of high drama.

James: I seriously thought I was going to go. It was because the dried flavour dust that coats the Tangy Tom got into my wet throat and moulded itself into where my throat hole was. I was watching something on telly, breathed in and it got lodged. It wasn't bloody funny! Be careful with them. They should come with a warning.

Clair: Maybe they should say: 'Cut them in half like you do with grapes for kids if your husband's a liability.'

James: Space Raiders are a safer option. They've got built-in air holes.

Clair: Ah, Space Raiders! What a classic. We have them all the time in this house.

James: But they cost a fortune these days.

Clair: I know, they're like 35p. It's a crime. But I'll still treat myself. Even the beef ones are brilliant.

James: They're not pickled onion though, are they?

Clair: That's fair. I'll tell you a terrible day in the confectionery world. When they stopped doing Taz bars.

James: A worse day was when they started charging you 30p for a Freddo. And in London I reckon you'd be lucky to see change out of 50p.

Clair: I remember when your mum used to give you a pound and you could get so much with it. Five packets of crisps or ten Chomps. If I gave Harrison a pound now, I don't think he'd be able to get more than one thing. Me and James talk about this a lot because we feel like we're the last generation where we had the old stuff that people talk about, like the 10p crisps. We didn't have mobile phones and the Internet was really new just as we were getting older. We still watched VHS videos but then DVDs were around the corner for us. I feel like we're the turning point generation.

James: I was leaving school when it was just starting to get usual to have a phone. I remember them being around before then but I wasn't a billionaire so it wasn't until I left school that it happened for me. And what a day that was.

Clair: The Nokia 3210 was the phone that everyone had, and that was the one with *Snake* on it. I remember wanting that more than anything else I'd ever seen in my life. I remember thinking, *If I just had that, I'd be the happiest person in the world*. That and a can of dandelion and burdock, which my papa used to drink, a can of Irn-Bru and a couple of bags of 10p crisps and you'd be away.

James: Gotta love a good can. But I'll tell you what I'm not a fan of. Sometimes you go to a posh do and they give you that fancy fruity water.

Clair: Elderflower.

James: That's it. It's out of order that is. They should say, 'By the way, that's not just plain water I've just given you' so you don't feel violated.

Clair: One of the worst things in the world is when you're at a wedding or a do and you reach for a glass of what you think is still water but it turns out to be bloody fizzy! It's the disappointment of not getting what you thought was on offer.

James: Nope, love a bit of fizzy stuff.

Clair: Also, I don't like white wine because it tastes like flat champagne. So it's the opposite but the same feeling.

James: You know what, I've never had white wine.

Clair: I'm not a big wine drinker. I like a bit of red, but only because I made myself like it, but white wine, yuk. One thing I like doing is adding salt and vinegar to a pack of Hula Hoops.

James: Yeah, they hold the moisture well so you

don't end up with a little puddle in the bottom corner. Be careful, that's all I'm saying.

Clair: You have to know what you're doing.

James: Don't f**k about.

Clair: When's the last time you saw an advert for crisps on telly?

James: Haven't seen Lineker in a while. And you don't see cereal ads do you? What's the Sugar Puff monster up to? How's Tony the Tiger getting along? Do you remember the Ready Brek advert?

Clair: The one with the little boy all glowing. I used to love Ready Brek in the winter.

James: Takes you back. I've got a weird thing about old adverts. I love 'em!

Clair: We did watch a lot of telly. We were either outside playing or inside watching telly in our house. There was no in-between. There weren't a lot of days out, going ice skating or a trip to the cinema. You were either in the park with your pals or inside with the telly on. And then for supper, the old white cans with nothing on them would come out the cupboard.

James: You know, a couple of years ago I was thinking of putting some merch out, just a white T-shirt with 'No Frills Baked Beans' printed on it in black.

Clair: That's quite good for *At Home with the Buckleys*, because we're all about the no frills!

I edit the vlog videos and it kind of makes sense for me to do it. James is very good with computers but he was doing his Twitch streams every day so he didn't really have time to edit the videos, so he showed me how to do the basics. And after that, I spent a lot of time looking up tutorials on how to do stuff while I was editing the videos. I learned on the job.

I used to worry about how many people were going to watch the channel. And then, when we first started it, anywhere between 200,000 and 800,000 were catching the vlogs. That seemed absolutely insane that that many people were watching us mess about on a couch! But James knew that this was a bit unusual and probably wouldn't last. He thought it was mainly because we released it during lockdown, so people were bored and they'd already watched everything on Netflix(!) before stumbling across our little channel.

So he thought it would level off after lockdown lifted and to be fair, he was right. But then we had a little bit of a dip in numbers after we started leaving the house in the vlogs. People seemed to just want to see us at home, and to be fair to them, that is the name of the channel. But a lot of the popularity of a video depends on YouTube and how the algorithms work and that stuff is just beyond me. As soon as a video gets on to the YouTube home page (as it did for us once with the 'Christmas is Cancelled' video), even if it's just for a minute, you'll end up with like a million views. But nobody knows how that happened and how we could do it again. You just put videos out and hope for the best! Well, we do anyway. There might be people who know what they're doing out there somewhere.

I'll watch every video again as soon as it goes live to check I haven't left anything weird in that James has said or kept the kids' faces in it, even though I've already watched it before then. But I get heart palpitations every time! It's a constant battle between you and the platform trying to figure out how to get the video noticed and what magic combination of keywords you need to come up with. It's a minefield. And I'm not sure I'm that great at it. We missed about three or four weeks (not in a row) and we noticed a dip then, so one thing I learned is that if you want to keep your numbers up and your audience happy, you've got to keep generating content each week. You have to be consistent. Which is fair enough. It's a very demanding relationship! It doesn't matter how big your channel is. If you switch off for a month, you can't expect people to be like 'Oh wow, they're back!' People move on. So many people ask us to do more videos a week and there might come a time when we do. We have a couple of ideas for some extra videos, little series of their own which we think our audience would enjoy, so stay tuned!

I can see from the data that our audience seems to be mostly married couples, some with young kids. But you can kind of tell who's watching you from the comments you get. And the question we get asked the most, without a doubt, is: 'What colour's your kitchen paint?' (From the old kitchen.) And the second one is more of a comment that goes something like: 'This is one of the very few things that me and my husband watch together'. And I love that one. It makes me so happy. I do get a lot of people telling me 'That's exactly what my husband/boyfriend is like' or 'My missus is so similar to you and I'm like James' etc., which does make me laugh.

So on that note, one of the things that James does (that drives me mental) is that rather than looking for something that I know (and he knows) we already have in the house or garage, he sometimes just buys a new one. And he did that not so long ago with a handheld hoover. I got really pissed off because I knew that the hoover we already have comes apart and becomes a handheld one. And James was like, 'But we could keep it upstairs'. So we ended up having an argument about it because I was annoyed that he was wasting money. Because in classic James fashion it wasn't just any old hand-held hoover, it was an extortionately expensive one! And we got it all on film. When I came to edit that vlog, I cut all of that out. James watched it and asked me where all the stuff was about the hoover. And I said, 'We can't put that in – I was genuinely pissed off!' But he was like, 'Trust me – people will love it! Put the hoover stuff back in.' So I did and we got so many comments saying 'That's exactly what my husband's like!' It resonated with people for the reason I edited it out – because it was real! I have found that YouTube is quite a friendly place compared with other social media apps. People are watching your videos because they like you and, yeah, you do get the odd comment but we don't get many bad ones at all.

I do really like reading the comments and taking the time to reply to people. I don't get anxious about what people are going to say in the way I used to do when something came out in the press about us when we were first together. And without sounding like a knob, it's great when people say things like 'Clair's my favourite' or 'Came here for James, stayed for Clair'. One person who messaged us in December 2021 told us he'd just found the channel and loved it. After catching up on all the episodes he said:

> From what I can gather, James doesn't understand why we watch these videos and why we like them but farts a lot. Clair loves to paint and decorate, gets annoyed by James a lot, great accent, loves Halloween and horror. Harrison and Jude, full of joy and very talented little boys, playing guitars etc. Paisley: a big dog that some people might be afraid of when out walking but is just a puppy at heart. Also, I've learned so much about Surfshark!

And I just thought that is so nice. One word that comes up a lot in comments is 'wholesome' which is amazing given that most of what we do is fart, swear, eat junk food and drink. We've had the comment that 'We're the Seinfeld of vloggers' a few times, which I love, and it kind of makes sense. I mean, we talk about nothing really but people seem to like it!

One thing I do get support about is the bane of my life – James's Mini. I actually hate it, everything about it. It's a horrendous purple, which makes it look like we're driving along in one of those big Quality Street sweets. And everyone looks at it, which is bad enough, but then they recognize James driving it, which is doubly annoying because we as a rule don't like to draw attention to ourselves, especially when we're out with the boys. It's so different to our family car, the Range Rover, where we can go around pretty much unnoticed (unless we've got the camera on in the car for the vlog, in which case everyone seems to turn up!) because it's quite a popular car. He got round me with that one giving me this spiel about how it's one of the safest cars so if I was out by myself with the boys and someone was to hit us, we'd be really safe. So I was like all right, fine. But it's meant now that I don't want to go in anything even vaguely dangerous (or stupid) like a Mini. Maybe my mum instincts take over!

The Mini wouldn't be so bad if it wasn't so ugly. But the amount of money, time and effort that's been poured into it...wow. After getting it fixed for about the thirtieth time, James was desperate to drive it so we drove it down to Brighton to see some friends. We got everyone in there, us and the boys, and it was a long, very bumpy drive. It was OK on the way there but the journey home wasn't fun. James couldn't control the steering for a bit so we started swerving around, which wasn't great. It's a never-ending saga, this bloody Mini.

But I don't think he'll ever get rid of it. So it fills up the garage, along with a treadmill that he never uses. I'm too easy on him. But maybe it's because I've chosen not to care too much about it. Whatever keeps him out of my hair!

The Art of the Fart

James: Farting is more than a pastime; it's a passion. A couple of people who watch the channel have even referred to me as a 'fartist', which I like because, you know what, it is an art form. And the master farter was a guy called Joseph Pujol (seriously, you can't make that name up), who made a career out of unique skills and went by the stage name Le Pétomane (which translates from French as 'farting maniac'). He was so good that he could fart famous pieces of music, including the French national anthem, which he'd perform at the Moulin Rouge in Paris. He got so popular that members of European royal families came to see him. It sounds like I've made all this up, but it's true! What a legend.

So influenced, I started categorizing farts for your enjoyment. Clair's gonna love these pages.

The Classic Parp – Short, sharp and deployed deliberately for comic effect.

The Down Under – Musical fart that goes up towards the end, much like an Aussie accent. It almost sounds like it's asking you a question.

The Squeaker – A fart that's been held in for too long and finally slips out apologetically in a soft but high-pitched whine that often keeps going.

The Fall Guy – One that has to come out but you've got someone you can blame it on: the dog.

The Welcome Release – A fart that's been stored up for some time, often in the cinema or theatre and is released to great relief upon leaving the auditorium.

The Crackler – A fart that relies on a leather sofa or armchair for reverberation and amplification. Used by a resourceful farter who's aware of their surroundings.

The Commando – Another site-specific fart deployed while walking up an escalator on the Tube to ensure the maximum number of casualties. Named after the ludicrous death toll in the Arnie movie.

The Unmentionable – Unexpected, unplanned fart from someone of advancing years or of high social standing who does not acknowledge what just happened. It's unclear whether or not they heard it but no one in the blast radius dares mention it. Everyone just continues what they were doing, pretending not to notice the waft invading their nostrils.

The Thunder Clap – A deep rumbling that strikes fear into people's hearts. You're not quite sure where it's come from but you know another's on the way.

The Wet One – A fart that often starts encouragingly but takes a sinister turn once the farter has already committed. Tends to cause an anxious glance in the direction of the nearest toilet.

The Marco Polo – Two skilled farters start a ping-pong farting session (pun fully intended) which can turn competitive. The results often speak for themselves but if it's a close-run thing, one usually honourably acknowledges the other's victory.

The Glancer – A skilled fartist can angle the fart off a surface to create a helpful ricochet that can transform a mediocre fart into something that makes you take notice. Indicates creativity, efficiency and prior planning. A thinker's fart.

The Silent But Violent – A classic for a reason. There's no warning sound, just quiet asphyxiation. Used to devastating effect in confined spaces. Difficult to identify the culprit.

The Aftershock – After the initial eruption come the quieter tremors. Much like a good horror story, it keeps your audience on edge.

The Cover-up – This fart sneaks out in a place where you can't be farting. And you're conscious that someone knows you've let one out so you try and cover it up by moving things around (a chair, your phone, your feet) that might make a similar sound. It never works.

Laughart – This one squeezes out accidentally when you're laughing really hard. But it's how you deal with the situation next that matters. If you go red and get embarrassed, the laughter will stop. But if you embrace it and keep laughing, you'll often find yourself rewarded with a bigger fart.

The Fart Fireworks – A skilled farter can command the attention of an audience, squeezing out parps of all shapes and sizes that continue for some time.

The Jack the Let Ripper – With this one, you're not even safe outside. It'll find you. But unlike the fart, the culprit soon flees into the wind.

The I Thought I Was Alone – This is one you've been saving up for the right moment. Perhaps you're in polite company, so you wait until you're by yourself, in the gents' toilet, maybe. Then you let rip, but just as you're about to, the door to the gents or one of the cubicles opens unexpectedly.

The I Thought It Was Safe – You've had a shocker with this one. You try and give it the beans but you only realize once you've committed that it's more than just wind you're passing. Named in honour of a well-known *Inbetweeners* scene.

On the subject of 'I Thought it was Safe', this happened to me in real life in May 2017, which is something I chose to share with the nation on *The Graham Norton Show* during an appearance with Ed Westwick promoting *White Gold*. I was working on the TV show *Zapped* during the week and coming home at the weekends to see Clair and the boys. One Sunday, just after we'd had a family dinner, it was coming towards the time I needed to leave and Harrison got really upset that I was going away already. But at that moment it felt like

I had a fart coming, and I thought, *This will cheer him up! He'll love this.* So I said, 'I'm sorry mate, I've gotta go, but come here and give me a big squeeze.' And I thought I'd pretend that he'd squeezed me too hard and let out a comedy fart, as you do. But he took a little bit longer to come over than I thought and I was losing the fart a bit. So I leaned over (Harrison was only five then) in a slightly awkward position and maybe pushed a bit too hard because before I knew it, I'd shit myself. And I did what you have to do in that situation when everyone's looking at you. 'Sorry guys, I've shit myself. I've gotta go for an emergency shower!' It happens people, and it's about time someone came out and spoke about it.

'We're not scum! We're scummy'

James: While we've been getting on with putting vlogs out almost every week, I have been up to other stuff (I'm not always playing video games upstairs). This is where I mention I've been in a play, in case you haven't heard.

Clair: So James was about to get a call from his agent telling him that a director wanted to talk to him about a part in *2:22: A Ghost Story*. So he went upstairs and took the call, came back downstairs and said 'I think I'm doing it. I just don't think it's something I can say no to.' I feel like James knows the stuff where he'll need to ask me if I'm all right with it, like when he got this part in *Charlie Countryman* (2013), a film with Shia LaBeouf that was being shot in Bucharest and would take a long time. He said, 'It's a good cast, Shia LaBeouf, Rupert Grint – big names – but it's gonna be a while and I won't be able to come home in between.' And I said, 'Look – you've got to do it'. So sometimes we'll have those conversations, and other times I know he'll have to do it and we'll just figure it out. *2:22* was one of those moments.

I can tell what James is feeling because he wears his heart on his sleeve (actors are like that), so I know when he's sad or happy but you can't really get that from me. I usually keep things to myself more and try to deal with them more quietly. On 2:22, you could tell that he was excited each day going in to work. I helped James with his lines for the play, highlighting the script where he had lines (such a wife thing to do, I know).

 **James**: Getting the role in *2:22: A Ghost Story* was a big deal for me. It was the first time I'd been on the West End stage since *Les Misérables* in 1999 at the Palace Theatre. It felt like the right thing to do. I'd been offered similar stuff in the past but I kept talking myself out of it. I think part of that was down to confidence and overthinking

things, but also because the prospect of the West End was just too nerve-wracking. When you're younger, the idea of putting on a Deep South accent, which I needed for *Whistle Down the Wind*, didn't phase me. I didn't think about it, I just said, 'Yeah, I'll give it a go.' But you get older, you start worrying about it. But it felt like the right time to reconnect with that feeling that I remember having played Gavroche in *Les Mis*. And being part of *2:22*, I've found that feeling again. All the ingredients were there, though. Everyone else was really good in it, it had already had a run that had been a success (starring Lily Allen, Julia Chan, Hadley Fraser and Jake Wood). It was just up to me to see if I could slot into that, take a chance and see if I could still pull off that kind of stuff.

The Covid thing before Christmas 2021 was a challenge and for a time we didn't know if shows would start getting cancelled, but we were one of the fortunate few productions that kept the wheels turning throughout. And the people that had seen it before Christmas had been telling their mates about it, because we saw big crowds for the performances after Christmas. My castmates are all just really good at what they do, and that makes you feel secure. Everyone that worked on it was brilliant. The director, Matt, is one of the best I've ever worked with, despite all the interval training exercises he made us do at the beginning.

Yes, it was stressful, but to be honest, I'm always stressed about something or another. The energy that gets used over a long period of time does just make you tired constantly, which you have to adjust to. On paper, it looks like you're just on stage for 2 hours a night, but there's so much work that goes into it. I wouldn't ever call it proper work though. For Elliot Cowan, who played Sam, this is what he does and he's an absolute pro at it. He's very relaxed, turns up, does the play, goes home and has a good night's sleep. My approach is slightly different. I'm very nervous, knacker myself after each performance, go home and can't sleep because I'm completely wired. The adrenaline keeps pumping and I don't fall asleep until gone 2am. Then I have to do it all again the next day, even more stressed and tired! See, Elliot, that's how you do it, son.

One of the great things about the play is that lots of people came to the show multiple times because once they found out the big twist, they wanted to hunt for the little clues you get along the way and make sense of them. So we were performing to quite a few people that had already really enjoyed it, so there was a lot of goodwill about. Also, it just feels like more of a film than a play and I can't think of anything else like it. It's more accessible than a lot of plays and you see a younger crowd in the theatre, so maybe this is one of those plays that attracts the next generation of theatregoers. They call the usual demographic the 'grey pound', which is the sort of folks you normally go after, but this has definitely got a wider appeal. I feel like *2:22* is for a different audience than normal plays. It feels like something that anyone can get on board with.

I loved working on the play but it definitely stretched me. It's really stressful possibly making some sort of major cock-up each night and not in a funny way. Living with that all the time does give you a heightened anxiety, which is knackering, but I can see myself doing more West End stuff in the future. I'd love to go back and do *Les Mis* again when I'm in my early forties. It's been a dream of mine for a while, to maybe go back as Javert this time. It'll stay on forever, that show, it's so good.

Finishing *2:22* was a difficult comedown because you get so used to spending every day with people and then suddenly you're doing your last performance and they're taking the set down before you know it. Stephanie (Beatriz) left a big hole, because she headed back to LA but the next time I'm over there (or us as a family are there), we'll all go to dinner and do something fun. But it's all swings and roundabouts. I'm writing this a few days after the run ended and I'm enjoying spending a few days not feeling like I'm going to have a heart attack at any second. And going to sleep before midnight. My sleep pattern was all over the place during *2:22*. I was getting home at 11pm every night but I was still shaking. I had a constant feeling of fight or flight and while I really enjoyed the experience, I felt like I'd been a kid at school who'd got into a fight every day. And for ten weeks, that's hard! We did have one person who had to be stretchered out of the perform-ance, but I had the blinkers on, concentrating on what I was doing and trying not to ruin it for everybody. I do get very angry with myself if I make a mistake because every night I want it to be the best show we can possibly do. And I know that's impossible and I'm kind of setting myself up to fail, but I can't help but approach my entire life that way. I constantly disappoint myself. I'm not doing anything as good as how I feel it should be, whether it's a TV show, West End production, writing something, keeping fit or BBQing a good bit of steak. I take everything to the extreme. It usually gets to a point where someone (Clair) has to take me to one side and ask 'James – what are you doing?' I just can't seem to do a bit of something. I just see how far I can take something and it's never far enough. Which is probably a good reason why I don't do drugs! It's an exhausting way to be, though, and I just realized this properly recently.

Anxiety is a double-edged sword. It can spur you on, make you double down and work really hard at something; but on the flip side, it's knackering and the moments of being satisfied are so fleeting. You always cross-examine if you could have done things differently or better or resolve to work harder next time. I'm not saving people's lives, but I do put so much pressure on myself. The only time I haven't felt like that was on *The Inbetweeners*, but don't get me wrong, there were days where I worried we weren't doing as good a job as we could have, but on the whole, most of that was just so much fun and it was a nice release not to feel the pressure I usually put on myself.

For the past few years, I've gone over to LA for pilot season, spent a couple of months there with Clair's family. Just being in the car on the way from LAX to Clair's aunt's house, you just find yourself marvelling at how the Americans make everything iconic, whether it's their cars, signposts or even just a coffee cup. They take something simple and turn it into a piece of art. And then you see it in an even bigger form on the big screen. Everything looks amazing in America. I remember trying to write something for a while with Karl Pilkington and we were talking about what we wanted to do. Being two working-class guys, we wanted to write about what that was like and the characters we grew up with. Karl thought it would be so much easier if we set it in the States because the American equivalent of a really depressing high-rise British council estate just looks more visually interesting and engaging on a screen. If you tried to do the British version of the opening credits of *The Sopranos* (where you see the journey from Manhattan into New Jersey), you'd be driving round the M25, which doesn't quite have the same glamour and romance.

When I do the LA trip I like travelling on a Sunday because it makes it easier to get to and from Heathrow. So I get a flight on Saturday night on the way back so I arrive in London on Sunday. It's just less stressful that way. But I'm not heading there in 2022. I'm going to take a bit of a break. Right now, it just makes sense for me in terms of what I want to do with my life and how I want to live it to pursue this YouTube adventure that me and Clair are doing now and see where that goes. I feel like I've been beaten into submission by the Internet so maybe I should embrace it and use it as a way to make a living! That's what I'm concentrating on at the moment. Although, I'm an actor first and if anything comes up that I can't say no to, I'll be happy to put the actor hat back on. Which to be honest, also makes good content for our channel. It's my job and our audience enjoy getting that little sneak back-stage of what it's like on a set or on a play. Hopefully soon I'll be able to take them all on to the set of something cool. *cough* Bond *cough*!

If I stream on Twitch, that's to an audience of maybe two thousand people and that's an audience I can handle. And they're people that have sought me out. Similarly, being in *2:22* was performing to an audience of around a thousand people who had bought tickets, wanted the show to be good and weren't there to heckle or ruin what's going on. That was such a joy to do, to feel appreciated and that people aren't out to get you. I just want to entertain people and make them happy, but even that can sometimes be tricky these days.

I always wanted to be a star in a hit sitcom, and I've been lucky enough to do it. I look back at *The Inbetweeners* with a mixture of emotions. I feel so privileged to have been a part of it but a bit sad that life isn't like that all the time. One of the things that came off the back of it, though, was casting agents and producers asking me what sort of stuff I want to do. And I got so obsessed with trying to find out the answer to that question. But I feel like I still don't know, and it's been eleven and a half years since the TV series ended. On the last night of *2:22*, one of the producers came up to me and asked me what I wanted to do next and I just said 'I don't know'. Hopefully, one day I'll wake up with an idea of what I want to do. Maybe it's time for me to retire and just sit in the house all day.

The Buckleys' Blackboard

The kitchen blackboard might be gone (didn't suit the new kitchen did it!), but it's not forgotten! We couldn't end this book without collecting together some of the... ermm... 'wisdom' we've shared in the vlogs, and you guys gave us some amazing suggestions. So here's a round-up of some of our favourite quotes that would have made it onto the blackboard!

Jonny Hobson

'You've f**ked it haven't you?' (James's comment on the haircut Clair did for him during lockdown.)

Belle Callaghan

'Listen to them, the children of the night. What music they make!' (*Dracula*)

Arran W

'All work and no play, makes Jack a dull boy.'

The Buckleys

'Hey Clair, it's vlog time, put down your gin, it's time to go to work!'

Raxyroobear

'We make up horrors to help us cope with the real ones.' (Stephen King)

mozza1878

'Just because you're paranoid, don't mean they're not after you.' (Kurt Cobain)

The Buckleys

'You're zooming right into my face. You can see the muck in my pores.'

Emma Watson (*not* that *Emma Watson*)

'No one ever made a difference by being like everyone else.' (P T Barnum)

Darren Bailey

'The greatest lesson in life is to know that even fools are right sometimes.' (Winston Churchill)

The Buckleys

'If it's one thing that we are, Clair, it's minimal.'

Maggie Malone

'I am a deeply superficial person.' (Andy Warhol)

fawcett7272

'If you want the rainbow you gotta put up with the rain.' (Dolly Parton)

Celyn284

'We all go a little mad sometimes.' (*Psycho*)

The Buckleys

'Trying to clean while the kids are at home all the time is like trying to brush your teeth while eating Oreos.'

Reece Thomas

'I'm having an old friend for dinner.' (*The Silence of the Lambs*)

Ian Welsh

'Double, double toil and trouble; Fire burn and cauldron bubble.' (*Macbeth*. And *Harry Potter*)

Vintage Belle

'Hell is empty and all the devils are here.' (*The Tempest*)

The Buckleys

'Shave me, put me in a school uniform and I'll be happy to do *The Inbetweeners* again.'

Kenny McClymont

'Artificial intelligence is no match for natural stupidity!' (Albert Einstein)

Simon David Harris

'No good story starts with a salad.'

S P

'I mean, we are nuts.' (Clair Buckley)

The Buckleys

'They say misery loves company. Well you're misery and I'm company.'

Baggies Joe

'Out of everything I've lost, I miss my mind the most!' (Ozzy Osbourne)

Kelly Hobbs

'As usual, there is a great woman behind every idiot.' (John Lennon)

Jane Ahlfeld

'You just have to trust your own madness.' (Clive Barker)

The Buckleys

'We're just a couple of common dirtbags. That's what people like about us.'

Phil Arnold

'I'm going to count to three. There will not be a four.' (Hans Gruber)

Phil Fiddler

'We're all mad here.' (*Alice in Wonderland*)

Don Keynote

'Never trust the living.' (*Beetlejuice*)

Ed Wiseman

'Every day is Halloween, isn't it? For some of us.'
(Tim Burton)

The Buckleys

'We're not scum, we're scummy.'

Clair: Does this book have an ending? Have we thought that far ahead?

James: I don't think we've ever really thought ahead about anything Clair.

Clair: Shall we just wing it then?

James: Yeah, probably. Well, let's give them a proper outro, like we do on the vlogs.

Clair: Ok. Good idea. Something snappy and hilarious. Always end on a joke.

[doorbell rings]

James: Forget it! Curry's here!

Clair: Bye guys, stay scummy!

Acknowledgements

Firstly, thank you to Briony Gowlett. Without her we would never have done this. To everyone at Octopus Publishing Group and Radar.

Thank you to Amy, Lucy, Robyn and Adam at Gleam for their support and advice through this process.

Huge thank you to Nathan Joyce, who took our ramblings, our mundane and insane stories, our conversations about nothing and our daft ideas of what was hilarious, and managed to shape them all into the form of a readable book.

To all our friends and family who have been so supportive of our new adventure of *At Home With The Buckleys*.

And to our little Harrison and Jude. Thank you for being the coolest little dudes on the planet. For making parenting, family life and adulthood in general a laugh-a-minute fun ride!